J. Ellard Gore

Planetary and stellar Studies

J. Ellard Gore

Planetary and stellar Studies

ISBN/EAN: 9783743330023

Manufactured in Europe, USA, Canada, Australia, Japa

Cover: Foto ©ninafisch / pixelio.de

Manufactured and distributed by brebook publishing software (www.brebook.com)

J. Ellard Gore

Planetary and stellar Studies

PREFACE.

THE following pages are chiefly reprints of papers published by the author during the last fifteen years in scientific and other periodicals, and in the proceedings of learned societies. Some of the papers have been partly re-written, and the information brought up to date. The following chapters have not been previously published—Mercury, the Minor Planets, Uranus, Neptune, and on the Distances of the Fixed Stars. It is hoped that this little work will be found to contain matter of interest both to the general reader and also to the more advanced student of Astronomy.

July, 1888.   J. E. G.

CONTENTS.

CHAP.		PAGE
I.	INTRODUCTION	13
II.	MERCURY	15
III.	VENUS	23
IV.	TRANSITS OF VENUS	32
V.	MARS	35
VI.	THE MINOR PLANETS	45
VII.	JUPITER	53
VIII.	SATURN	67
IX.	URANUS	75
X.	NEPTUNE	81
XI.	DOUBLE STARS	87
XII.	VARIABLE STARS	93
XIII.	NEBULÆ	103
XIV.	ON THE DISTANCES OF THE FIXED STARS	115
XV.	THE MILKY WAY	125
XVI.	THE GREAT PYRAMID AND THE PROCESSION OF THE EQUINOXES	129
XVII.	CHANGES IN THE STELLAR HEAVENS	137
XVIII.	THE NEW STAR IN ORION	161
XIX.	THE VARIABLE STAR MU CEPHEI	167

CHAP.		PAGE
XX.	ON THE PROBABLE VARIABILITY OF BETA LEONIS	171
XXI.	ON THE MASSES AND DISTANCES OF BINARY STARS	177
XXII.	ON THE ABSOLUTE DIMENSIONS OF A STAR CLUSTER	185
XXIII.	SOME SUSPECTED VARIABLES OF THE ALGOL TYPE	193
XXIV.	ON THE POSITIONS OF THE PLANES OF BINARY STARS	201
XXV.	STELLAR PHOTOGRAPHY	209
XXVI.	THE ZODIACAL LIGHT	217
XXVII.	THE INFINITY OF SPACE	233

APPENDIX.

Notes on the Planets	241
Binary Stars	245
Algol	248
Stellar Parallax	250
Binary Star Orbits	251
On the Magnitudes of Double Stars	253
On the Colours of the Components of Binary Stars	257
Classification of the Variable Stars	260

LIST OF ILLUSTRATIONS.

	PAGE
SATURN. Drawn by Henry Pratt, F.R.A.S.	*Frontispiece*
SATURN. Rings seen edgeways	68
MERCURY. Drawn by W. F. Denning, F.R.A.S. ...	16
VENUS AS A MORNING STAR. Drawn by W. F. Denning, F.R.A.S.	24
PHASES OF VENUS as viewed from the Earth ...	26
MARS. Chromo-litho, six views in three colours, two plates. Drawn by N. E. Green, F.R.A.S.	38
MARS. Snow Cap on South Pole. Drawn by N. E. Green, F.R.A.S....	40
PATH OF MARS. Drawn by R. A. Proctor, F.R.A.S.	36
JUPITER. Drawn by W. F. Denning, F.R.A.S. ...	54
MARKINGS ON JUPITER. Drawn by W. F. Denning, F.R.A.S.	57
RED SPOT ON JUPITER. Drawn by T. G. Elger, F.R.A.S.	61
PATH OF NEPTUNE. Drawn by R. A. Proctor, F.R.A.S.	82
TEMPORARY STAR OF 1572	138
NEW STAR IN CYGNUS (1876)	155

My best thanks are due to the Council of the Royal Astronomical Society, the Council of the Liverpool Astronomical Society, and to Messrs. Denning, Elger, Green, and Pratt for permission to reproduce some of the illustrations given.

J. E. G.

I.

INTRODUCTION.

THE study of the heavens has been since the earliest historical times a subject of interest to man. The Egyptians and Chaldeans watched the stars by night, and the Chinese annals of astronomy carry us back to a very remote antiquity. Most of their observations have proved to have been correct if we make allowance for the very imperfect methods of observation at their disposal. The telescope, that wonderful instrument of research, was not then invented, and they were obliged to trust to their powers of eyesight for their knowledge of the celestial bodies. Since the invention of the telescope thousands of stars and nebulæ previously unknown have been revealed to our gaze, the number of nebulæ alone now known to exist exceeding the number of stars visible to ordinary eyesight, so that if all the visible, or lucid stars, as they are called, were blotted out, thousands and millions of suns and systems would still remain to testify to the power of an Almighty Creator. The vast subject of astronomy may be divided into two heads—Planetary Astronomy, which treats of the planets, comets, and meteorites belonging to the Solar System, the system of which our earth forms a member; and Sidereal Astronomy, which takes a higher flight, and deals with suns belonging to other systems, each of them possibly as extensive as our own system, all probably forming one vast system, governed by laws and motions which at present we know little about, but which future scientific research will doubtless reduce to order and regularity. So far as is at present known the theory of gravitation appears to hold undisputed sway throughout the universe, all the observed motions in the so-called "fixed stars" being attributable to its power and regulated by its laws.

MERCURY.

MERCURY AS A MORNING STAR, NOVEMBER, 1882 (W.F.D.)

1. Nov. 5th, 18h. 50m.   2. Nov. 6th, 18h. 55m.
3. Nov. 8th, 19h. 30m.   4. Nov. 9th, 19h. 39m.
(10-inch Reflector, power 252.)

THE PLANETS.

II.

MERCURY.

MERCURY, the planet nearest to the sun, so far as yet ascertained, although rarely visible to the naked eye, was known to the ancients; the earliest recorded observation of the planet dating back to B.C. 264. It performs its revolution round the sun in a period of 87 days, 23 hours, 15 minutes, and 44 seconds. Of all the larger planets its orbit deviates most from the circular form, the eccentricity of the ellipse amounting to 0·2055, or, in other words, the distance of the sun from the centre of the ellipse described by Mercury is about $\frac{1}{5}$th of the semi-axis major (In the case of the earth's orbit this proportion is only $\frac{1}{60}$). Owing to this large eccentricity the difference between its greatest and least distances from the sun amounts to over 14 millions of miles, and consequently from this cause alone, the heat and light received by the planet from the sun when at its least distance will be more than double that at its greatest distance, this great change occurring in the space of about six weeks! The plane of Mercury's orbit is inclined to the plane of the ecliptic at an angle of about 7 degrees, which is greater than that of any of the other large planets. Its apparent diameter, as seen from the earth, varies from about 13 seconds to $4\frac{1}{2}$, and its mean diameter as seen from the sun is about 17·3 seconds, or nearly as much as that of the earth.[1] Its real diameter is about 3000 miles, so that in volume the earth is about 19 times larger. In density, however, Mercury is very heavy, its specific gravity being about seven times that of water (see Appendix, Note A). Schröter considered the flattening of the globe at the poles as insensible, and Sir William Herschel found it perfectly round in its transit over the sun's disc in 1802, but Simms in 1832 made the ellipticity $\frac{1}{17\cdot3}$, and Dawes in 1848 gave it $\frac{1}{25}$. The period of rotation, or the length of its day, has not been well ascertained. Bessel and Schröter agree in fixing it at about 24 hours, but the identity of this period with that of the earth looks suspicious, and Sir W. Herschel could not confirm the result arrived at by Schröter. During the transit of Mercury over the sun's disc on May 5, 1832, Schenck thought he observed a satellite near the planet, but this proved to be a sun spot, and was

[1] This is nearly true for Saturn also.

remarked by other observers. Transits of Mercury are more numerous than those of Venus, but are not so useful for obtaining the sun's distance from the earth. They always happen either in May or November. The last occurred on November 7, 1881, and the next will take place on May 10, 1891 (ending a little after sunrise in this country), and on November 10, 1894 (commencing a little before sunset), making a total of thirteen during the nineteenth century.

Mercury presents phases similar to those of Venus and the moon, and it has been occasionally noticed that the breadth of the illuminated portion is sometimes less than theory would require. At the transit of 1802 Sir W. Herschel could see no trace of any atmosphere. Other observers have, however, seen a luminous ring round the planet during transits in recent years, and in all probability an atmosphere of some kind does exist.

Some observers have concluded from the alternate blunting of the horns, when the planet is in the crescent form, that mountains of over 10 miles in height exist on its surface! but this seems very doubtful. Others have recorded dark streaks and spots on the planet, notably Schröter in 1801, Prince in 1867, Birmingham in 1870, Vogel 1871, and Schiaparelli in 1882. According to Denning, the markings on Mercury are much more easily seen than those on Venus, and even suggest an analogy to the markings on Mars. As the elongation of the planet from the sun seldom exceeds 18 degrees, it is a difficult object, at least in this country, to see without a telescope, and its disc

> "Can scarce be caught by philosophic eye
> Lost in the near effulgence of his blaze."

It is said that Copernicus, when on his death-bed, lamented that he had never been able to catch a glimpse of the planet, but his failure was probably due to the unfavourable nature of the climate in which he lived. Tycho Brahé was, however, more fortunate, and records several observations of Mercury with the unaided vision. The planet can occasionally be caught in this country with the naked eye after sunset, when favourably placed for observation, and I have so seen him several times in Ireland, the last occasion being on February 19, 1888, when I found the planet very visible in strong twilight near the western horizon, and apparently much brighter than an average star of the 1st magnitude would be if placed in the same position. In the clear air of the Punjab sky I observed Mercury on November 24, 25, 26, 27, 28, and 29, 1872, near the western horizon after sunset. Its appearance was that of a reddish star of the 1st magnitude. On November 29 I compared its brilliancy with that of Saturn, which was some distance above it, and making allowance for the glare near the horizon in which

Mercury was immersed, its lustre appeared to me to quite equal that of Saturn. In June, 1874, I found it about equal to Aldebaran, and of very much the same colour. Denning, who has seen Mercury with the naked eye about fifty times in England, estimated it on November 5, 1882, in the morning sky, as brighter than Sirius! He found its light sensibly decreased on November 6, but on November 8 it was still brighter than Arcturus.

In 1878, when Mercury and Venus were in the same field of view of the telescope, Nasmyth found that Venus was at least twice as bright as Mercury, and Zöllner found that, from a photometric point of view, the surface of Mercury is comparable with that of the moon.

VENUS.

VENUS AS A MORNING STAR, NOVEMBER, 1887 (W.F.D.)
1. Nov. 2nd, 6h. 30m. a.m.   2. Nov. 3rd, 7h. a.m.
3. Nov. 5th, 7h. a.m.   4. Nov. 6th, 7h. 30m. a.m.
(10-inch Reflector, power 252.)

III.

VENUS.

> "For a breeze of morning moves
> And the planet of Love is on high,
> Beginning to faint in the light that she loves
> On a bed of daffodil sky,
> To faint in the light of the sun she loves,
> To faint in his light and to die."
>
> TENNYSON.

THIS brilliant planet is, with the exception of the moon, our nearest neighbour in the Solar System. It was of course well known to the ancients. It is alluded to by Job (chap. xxxviii. 7), and probably by Isaiah (chap. xiv. 12). It is also mentioned by Hesiod, Homer, Virgil, Martial, and Pliny, and an observation of Venus is found on the Nineveh tablets of date B.C. 684. It was observed in daylight by Halley in July, 1716. The orbit it describes round the sun differs very little from a circle, less indeed than that of any other of the sun's family of planets. It revolves round the sun in a period of about 225 of our days at a mean distance of about 66 millions of miles, and in an orbit inclined to the plane of the ecliptic at an angle of 3 degrees, 23½ minutes. In size it is only a little smaller than the earth, its diameter being about 7,510 miles. In density it is about 5¼ times as heavy as water.[1] The flattening at the poles is generally considered as insensible. As well as can be ascertained by watching the motion of some faint spots on its surface, it has been concluded that the period of rotation, or the length of its day,

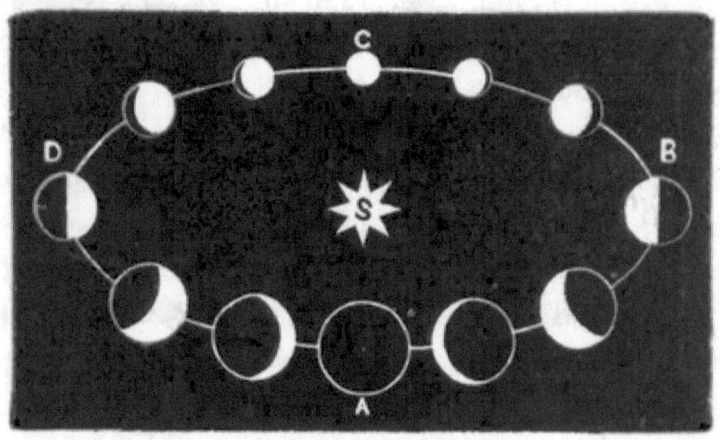

PHASES OF VENUS.

is a little less than that of the earth, but this is still very doubtful. It was called by the ancients Hesperus when an evening star, and Lucifer when a morning star. Venus exhibits phases similar to those of the moon, and these may be seen with a telescope of very small power. Their discovery— made by Galileo with an instrument of his own construction—was one of the first fruits of the telescope,

[1] See Appendix, Note B.

and confirmed the truth of the Copernican theory that the planets revolve round the sun, and not round the earth, as had been previously supposed. When near inferior conjunction, that is, when the planet is nearly between the sun and earth, Venus shows a crescent shape, similar to the moon when only a few days old. When at its greatest elongation from the sun, the phase is nearly that of the moon at "first quarter." When on the opposite side of its orbit it shows a nearly full face, but of course small, owing to its greater distance from the earth. At the time of its greatest brilliancy Venus can be distinctly seen with the naked eye in full sunshine, if its position in the sky is accurately known. The present writer has seen it well in India without optical aid half-an-hour before sunset, and when darkness sets in it casts a perceptible shadow. Olbers found that Venus, at its greatest brilliancy, is 19 to 23 times as bright as Aldebaran. G. P. Bond found it nearly 5 times the brightness of Jupiter. Plummer makes it 9 times that of Sirius, and Chacornac found her brightness to be 10 times greater than that of the most luminous parts of the moon. The surface of the planet is of such intense brilliancy that, although a fascinating object to the naked eye, it is rather disappointing in the telescope, exaggerating as it does all the faults of the lenses, and, indeed, none but the most perfect telescopes will define it clearly.

When Venus is in the crescent form, many observers have thought they could see the unilluminated portion of the disc, in the same way that the dark part of the moon is visible when only a few days old. This phenomenon, easily explained in the case of the moon by sunlight reflected from the earth, is wholly unaccountable in the case of Venus, and some astronomers ascribe it to an optical illusion. It was, however, noticed as early as the year 1715, and it has been often seen of late years by such excellent observers as Browning, Franks, Elger, Erck, Webb, and Winnecke. It is said to have been seen even in the day-time by Andreas Mayer, in October, 1759, and by Winnecke in September, 1871. As an attempt at a solution of the mystery a comparison has been suggested with some of our terrestrial nights which are much brighter than others, due to a phosphorescent glow over the whole sky, which has been noticed by Arago, Schröter, Webb, and by the present writer both in this country and in India.

Some recent observations of Venus may be mentioned. According to the Rev. S. H. Saxby, who observed the planet from February to October, 1884, the "dichotomy" of the disc, or the exact half-moon phase, did not occur exactly at the times of greatest elongation, as it should do according to theory, but about 6 days before eastern elongation, and 6 days after western elongation. Similar observations were recorded by the eminent German astronomers Beer and Mädler in 1836. The face of the planet was seen patchy or mottled by Gemmill in March, April, and May, 1884, and by Franks in October. The dark portion of the planet was also seen in 1884 by Franks and Perkins; darker than the sky by the former observer, and brighter than the sky by the latter, but Saxby failed to see any trace of the dark side. Some trace of this *lumière cendrée*, as it is called by French astronomers, was also seen by another observer Mr. J. M. Offord, who describes it as of a "Prussian blue colour." Denning says, "The only markings that seem distinguishable on Venus and which apparently survive repeated scrutiny are faint, grey areas without definite outlines. They are indeed so delicate in their visible aspect that the observer has difficulty in attributing their forms and positions, and will sometimes regard their very existence as of doubtful character." He finds that Venus is much whiter than Mercury, which has a rosy tinge, but thinks that the reddish colour of Mercury may possibly be due to the vapours near the horizon through which it is usually observed.

Venus was a brilliant object in the morning sky in November and December, 1887, and for some unaccountable reason was looked upon by the general public as a return of the "Star of Bethlehem"! It is almost needless to say that there is no foundation whatever for this idea. The star of the Magi was certainly not Venus. It may have been a "temporary star," but much more probably was quite a miraculous phenomenon.

Observations by Cassini, Mädler, Noble, and others seem to show that Venus is surrounded by a dense atmosphere, which according to Neison is nearly twice as dense as our own, and the luminous ring visible in transits of Venus over the sun's disc confirms this conclusion (see next article). The transits of Venus which occur at long intervals have been used for the purpose of calculating the earth's distance from the sun, but the experience derived from the transits of 1874 and 1882 has shown that a more exact knowledge of this very important element will probably in future be more accurately derived from observations of Mars, or some of the largest of the numerous small planets revolving between Mars and Jupiter.

Several observations are on record of a supposed satellite of Venus, but on account of its not being visible on so many other occasions on which the planet has been observed by astronomers, the matter has been termed "an astronomical enigma." M. Houzeau of the Brussels Observatory has recently attempted to explain the recorded observations by the hypothesis that the small body observed near Venus was in reality, not a satellite at all, but a small planet revolving round the sun in an orbit lying between the earth and Venus, and he provisionally named the planet "Neith"—the Egyptian Minerva—who was never seen behind her veil. Other astronomers, however, do not coincide with this view, and one writer has shown that the observations cannot be reconciled in the way M. Houzeau proposes. Since the publication of Houzeau's ingenious theory, the subject has been further studied by M. Paul Stroobant, who has come to the conclusion that in most of the recorded observations of a satellite, the object seen was really a fixed star. Thus Horrebow evidently observed θ Libræ, and Rœdkiœr seems on different occasions to have observed χ^4 Orionis, ν Geminorum, and m Tauri, which being brighter than the 5th magnitude might easily be seen when close to the planet. He rejects some of the observations, as probably due to the inferior quality of the telescope used, and finds that the only observations left unexplained by this theory are those made at Copenhagen in March, 1764. In some cases it is possible that one of the brighter asteroids may have been near Venus at the time of the observation. Thus this subject, which has been for so many years an enigma to astronomers, has now, at least to a considerable extent, been satisfactorily explained, and we may therefore conclude that Venus has no satellite, at least large enough to be visible with our present telescopes.

IV.

TRANSITS OF VENUS.

THE transit of Venus in December, 1874, was well seen by me in the Punjab, India, the sky being beautifully clear during the whole duration. With a 3-inch refractor, I could see nothing of the so-called "black drop" at ingress. At egress, a very small ligament was formed a few seconds before the internal contact. At ingress I distinctly saw the disc of Venus outside the sun's limb, owing to a faint ring of light which surrounded it, caused probably by refraction through the planet's atmosphere. While the planet was on the sun I could not see any light on the disc, nor any trace of a halo round the planet, which seems to have been noticed during the transit of 1769 by some observers. No trace whatever of a satellite was visible in my instrument with a power of 133 diameters.[1]

I observed the transit of December 6, 1882, in the West of Ireland, with the same 3-inch refractor.

[1] "Astronomical Register," Feb., 1875.

The sky was clear and the weather frosty, but the sun's limb, as seen in the telescope, was unsteady and "boiling" a good deal. Before external contact I could see no trace of Venus outside the sun. The planet was first seen forming a very small notch on the sun's limb. For some minutes before internal contact the arc of light round the disc of Venus (outside sun's limb) was well seen. This arc is caused by the refraction of the sun's light through the planet's atmosphere (and was well seen by me in India, during the transit of 1874). As the internal contact approached, this arc of light appeared to merge into the light of the sun's disc, and did not seem to interfere much with the appearance of geometrical contact, which seemed to me to be complete several seconds before a thread of the sun's light was seen outside Venus. Owing to the "boiling" at the sun's limb, the exact moment of the completion of this thread of light was very uncertain. I could see no trace whatever of anything resembling a "black drop." The disc of Venus was intensely and uniformly black, no trace of any light being visible on the disc, though I carefully looked for it. I could see nothing of a satellite. I saw the planet distinctly with the naked eye through a dark glass shortly after ingress. There were very few spots visible on the sun—a small group near the centre, and a small spot near the eastern limb.

MARS.

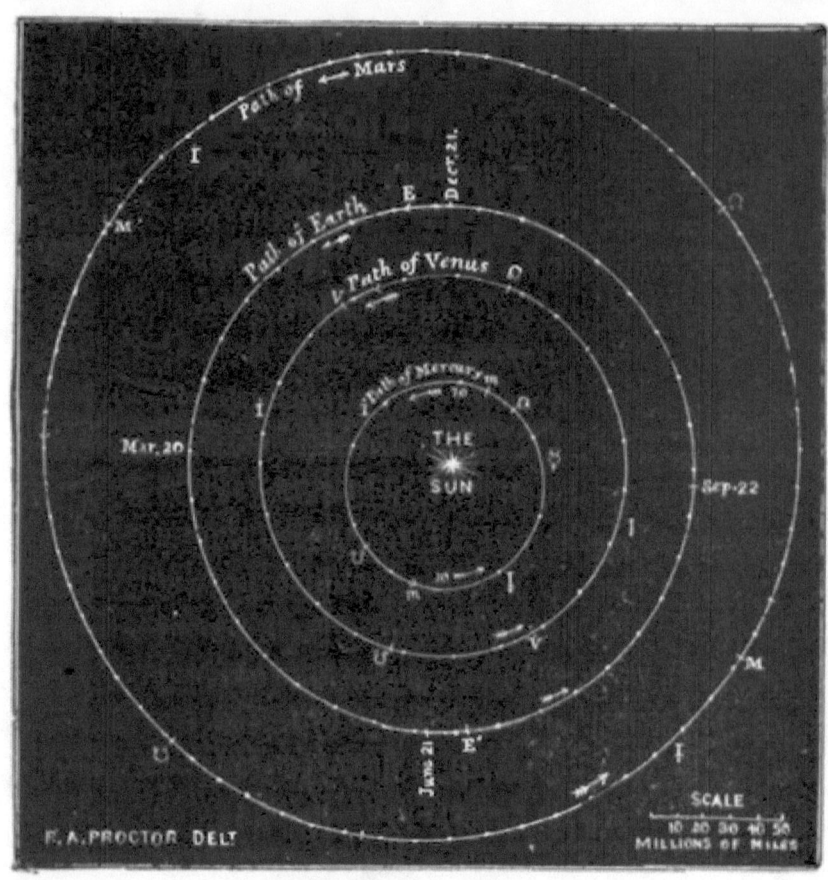

PATH OF MARS.

V.

MARS.

Mars, the red planet, as it is sometimes called, has been known since the earliest times. Aristotle speaks of an occultation of the planet by the moon, for which Kepler fixed the date April 4, 356 B.C. It is the next planet exterior to the earth in the Solar System, and revolves round the sun at a mean distance of about 139 millions of miles in a period of about 687 of our days. The eccentricity of its orbit is considerable (0·093), larger than that of any of the Major Planets, with the exception of Mercury. This brings the planet at one time of its year some 26 millions of miles nearer the sun than when at the opposite point of its orbit, and it has also the effect of bringing the planet nearer to the earth in some years than in others.

The diameter of Mars is about 4,200 miles, but the exact amount is somewhat doubtful. The flattening of its globe at the north and south poles seems from recent measures to be either very small or insensible.

In volume the earth is about seven times as large as Mars. In density also Mars is only three times as heavy as water, or but little more than half that of the earth.

Mars when in quadrature shows a gibbous phase, but when in opposition to the sun it exhibits a round full face like the full moon. These phases were discovered by Galileo, and prove that the planet shines by reflected light from the sun. When in opposition and at its nearest to the earth, as it was in 1877, and will be again in 1892, it rivals Jupiter in brightness, and its brilliancy combined with its red colour makes it, at these times, quite a conspicuous object in the heavens.[1]

The period of rotation or the length of the days on Mars has been determined with considerable accuracy. Cassini in 1666 found it to be 24 hours 40 minutes, but calculations made in recent years by the following astronomers, Kaiser, Wolf, Proctor, Schmidt, Marth, Denning, and Bakhuyzen, all agree in fixing it at about 24 hours, 37 minutes, $22\frac{1}{2}$ seconds, the only difference being in the decimal figures in the seconds! The attainment of such a degree of accuracy in the determination of the rotation period of this far-off world may appear to some impossible, but the calculation is an exceedingly simple one. An observation by Christian Huygens of a well-defined spot on its surface known

[1] See Appendix, Note C.

to astronomers as the Kaiser sea is on record. He found this spot to be centrally placed on the disc at a certain hour on Dec. 1, 1659. Now if we observe at any time the exact minute when this spot is situated exactly on the centre of the disc we have all that is necessary (neglecting some refinements) for our calculation. For, knowing roughly the length of the period, which can be obtained from a few weeks' observations, all we have to do is to divide this period into the number of seconds which have elapsed since the date of Huygen's observation. This will give us the number of rotations which have taken place in the interval between the two observations. Then dividing this number into the number of seconds in the interval, we obtain the rotation period to within a fraction of a second.

Examined with a good telescope, numerous spots are visible on the surface of Mars, evidently denoting the existence of land and water. These markings have been carefully mapped by Green and Proctor in England, and Burton and Dreyer in Ireland, and their delineations agree substantially in all the principal features, though differing slightly in some of the minor details. These maps show that the areas of land and water in Mars are about equal, while on the earth the water surface exceeds the land in the proportion of 3 to 1. In the year 1878, the eminent Italian astronomer, Schiaparelli observed a number of curious narrow streaks on the surface which he termed "canals." The existence of these strange features has been recently confirmed by the observations of Perrotin and Thollon, made at the Nice Observatory. They find that "in the equatorial region of the planet the so-called canals seem to form a complicated network of delicate grey lines extending in all directions, many of them being double, and exhibiting a remarkable parallelism."[1]

SOUTH POLE OF MARS.

Near the poles of Mars white spots are visible, which are considered to be snow-caps. This theory is supported by the fact that these white spots are observed to decrease in size during the Martial summer, and to increase again in winter. The existence of snow would of course imply the existence of an atmosphere. It seems to be a popular idea that the red colour of the planet is due to its

[1] "Journal of Liverpool Astronomical Society," vol. v. p. 67.

MARS. 1877.

MARS. 1877.

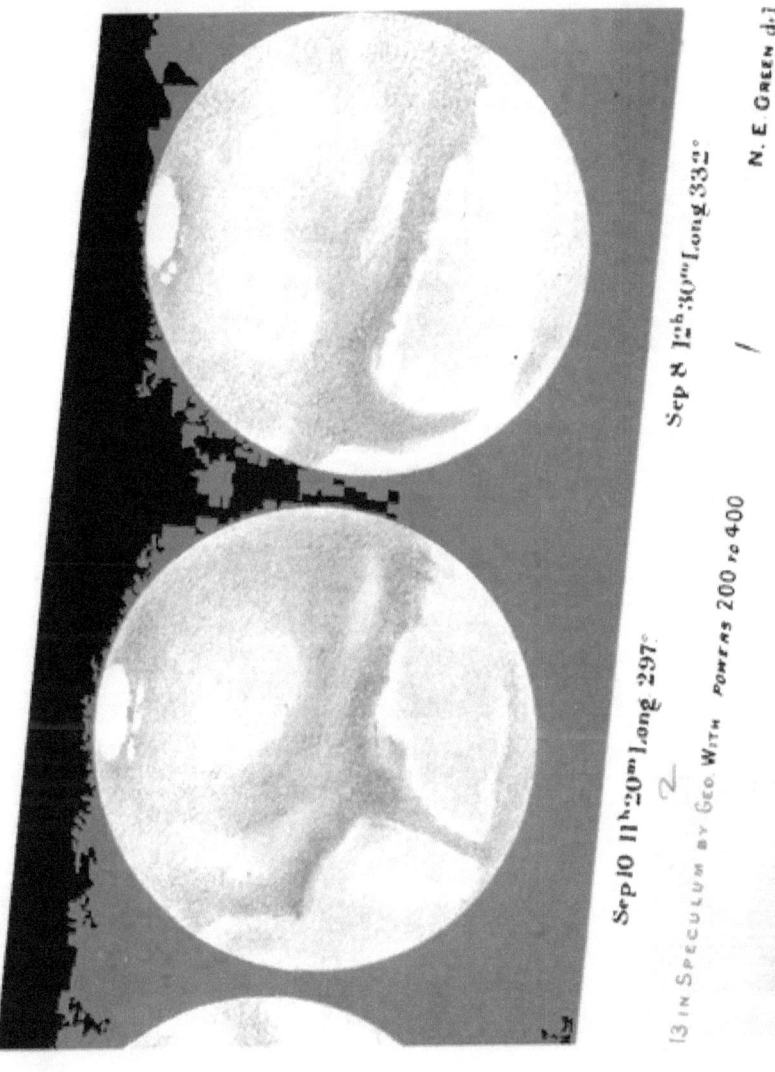

dense atmosphere, but observation shows that the atmosphere cannot be very dense, and as the colour of the polar snow-caps is not affected, it appears much more probable that the ruddy colour of Mars is due to the nature of its soil.

That Mars possesses an atmosphere similar to that of the earth we know from the fact that occasionally the markings on its surface are obscured from view by patches of white light which are evidently masses of clouds. These, if watched, often melt gradually away, showing the clearing up of the Martial skies. Some years ago the well-known astronomer, Lockyer, was observing Mars one night with a powerful telescope, and noticed that a well-known marking on its surface was partially hidden by a great white cloud. Another observer, the celebrated Dawes, was examining the planet on the same evening, and noticed the same peculiarity, but waiting for some hours longer, he succeeded in making a good drawing of the planet, which showed well the marking which had been previously obscured. It was literally a case of

"Wait till the clouds roll by."

It has also been observed that the hemisphere passing through the Martial summer is always more clearly seen than the other hemisphere in which winter reigns, showing that, as on earth the winter skies are more cloudy than those of summer.

Evidence of obscuration by cloud has also been recently observed by Perrotin and Thollon at the Nice Observatory.

According to Marth a transit of the earth and moon across the sun's disc as seen from Mars, occurred on Nov. 12, 1879.

Until lately Mars was supposed to have no satellites, and Tennyson with his usual scientific accuracy referred to the "snowy poles of moonless Mars." In 1877, however, Professor Hall, observing with the great 26-inch refractor of the Washington Observatory, most unexpectedly discovered two small satellites. These are very faint objects, and can only be seen with the largest telescopes, and when Mars is favourably situated for telescopic observation. They have been named Phobos and Deimos, and revolve round Mars nearly in the plane of the planet's equator. The smaller of the two, Deimos, is supposed not to exceed 6 miles in diameter; truly a miniature planet! It would not be a very long walk (about 19 miles) to start from any point on its surface, and walk round this "pocket planet." The diameter of Phobos is probably only 7 miles. These little moons revolve round Mars with such rapidity and of course in the same direction as the planet rotates on its axis, that the innermost Phobos actually rises in the *West*, and sets in the *East* three times during the course of the Martial day, and so close are they to the planet that they will be frequently subject to total eclipse, and will not be of much service as "torch-bearers" to the inhabitants of Mars, if any there be. Their small size will also render them ineffectual in the production of tides in the Martial oceans.

The inclination of Mars' axis of rotation to the plane of the orbit is, according to Schiaparelli, 65 degrees 48 minutes, or very similar to that of the earth, and taking further into consideration the distribution of land and water, the length of its day, and its atmosphere, the planet seems well fitted for the abode of living creatures.

THE MINOR PLANETS.

VI.

THE MINOR PLANETS.

The absence of a planet in the wide space between Mars and Jupiter was remarked by Kepler. This gap was first filled by the discovery of Ceres by Piazzi on the first day of the nineteenth century, Jan. 1, 1801. This was followed by the discovery of Pallas by Olbers in 1802, Juno by Harding in 1804, and Vesta by Olbers in 1807. No more were discovered till the year 1845, when Astræa was added to the list by Hencke, and Hebe by the same observer in 1847. Since that year fresh discoveries have been made annually, and now (1888)[1] the number of these small planets amount to 278. They are known by names as well as numbers. The mean distances from the sun vary from 2·133 (Medusa 149) times the earth's mean distance from the sun to 3·952 (Hilda 153) times that distance. Their periods of revolution round the sun vary from about $3\frac{1}{4}$ to $6\frac{3}{4}$ years. The orbits vary much in shape; some like Lomia (117), and Philomena (196),

[1] July, 1888.

being nearly circular, while others are very elliptical, like Æthra (132), of which the eccentricity is 0·38 and Istria (183), 0·353. Their inclination to the plane of the ecliptic also vary considerably; from that of Pallas, of which the inclination is about 34° 42', and Istria (183), 26° 30' to that of Massilia (20), which is only 0° 41', and Garumna (180), 0° 53'. Professor Kirkwood finds that the average eccentricity of the first 264 asteroids is 0·157, which is nearly equal to the mean eccentricity of Mercury, and exceeds that of any other of the large planets. He also finds that the mean inclination of the orbits to the ecliptic is about 8°.

There are gaps or vacant spaces in the zone of asteroids which have been explained by Kirkwood (and confirmed by Dr. Meyer and General Parmentier) as due to the disturbing action of Mars and Jupiter, especially the latter planet. The principal gaps are found to occur at the distances where an asteroid's period would be $\frac{1}{2}$, $\frac{1}{3}$, $\frac{3}{5}$, and $\frac{2}{5}$ of that of Jupiter. These gaps are similar to the divisions in Saturn's rings, which Dr. Meyer has shown to be due to the disturbing action of the satellites.

The minor planets vary greatly in brightness, and therefore probably in size. The brightest is Vesta, which sometimes reaches the 6th magnitude, and may be seen with the naked eye. Ceres is also said to have been seen in the same way, although it rarely exceeds the 7th magnitude. According to

Stone, the real diameters of the first 71 asteroids varies from 214 miles in the case of Vesta (4) to only 17 miles in the case of Echo (60)[1] Little or nothing is known about the physical condition of these small bodies. By careful observations of seven of them with a Zöllner photometer, Dr Müller finds that Vesta, Iris, Massilia, and Amphitrite only vary in brightness—like Mars—as the planet approaches opposition. On the contrary, he finds that Ceres, Pallas, and Irene vary in brightness as they vary in phase, similar to the moon or Mercury.

Sir John Herschel says: "A man placed on one of them would spring with ease 60 feet high, and sustain no greater shock in his descent than he does on the earth by leaping a yard. On such planets giants might exist; and those enormous animals which on earth require the buoyant power of water to counteract their weight might there be denizens of the land." A writer in Chambers's "Edinburgh Journal" some years ago, speaking of the probable dimensions of Astræa, says: "Think of this tight little island (Great Britain) wheeling along in independent fashion through space with all its proper features of vegetation and of animated being, a perfect miniature of those respectably sized orbs of which our own is a specimen. And supposing there are men and women upon it, think of the miniatures of nations which they must compose, and of all their

[1] See Note D.

other social arrangements in proportion. In that case, a piece of land the size of four or five English counties will be a goodly continent, and a mass of sea like the Frith of Forth a perfect Mediterranean. Rutlandshire would be a large addition to the Russian Empire in Astræa. The more common-sized kingdoms would be about the magnitude of our ordinary parishes. Perhaps the inhabitants may be characterized by more modesty than their earthly brethren; and it may have happened that when first they learned from their Copernicuses, Newtons, and Herschels, how matters really stood in the universe that they felt extremely abashed and disheartened about it. Let us for a moment imagine them fully persuaded that Astræa was the world, and that all the luminous bodies which, like us, they see in the sky were merely a drapery hung up for the regalement of their eyesights. What a mighty thing Astræa is, and what a grand set of beings are the Astræans! A sun to give us warmth and vegetation. Stars to begem our nightly view. Sister Pallas or Vesta occasionally sailing pretty close by, about the size of a moon, as if by way of a holiday spectacle. Everything very nice and complete about us. But, lo! astronomy begins to tell strange tales. It now appears that there are co-ordinate bodies called planets, probably inhabited as well as ours, and of infinitely larger size. The stars, morever, are suns, having other planets in attendance upon them, and these probable residences for human beings too. All at once Astræa shrinks from its position as the centre and principal mass of the universe into the predicament of a paltry atom hung loosely on to a machine whose centre is far otherwise. And the Astræans—the people of the world, the metropolitans of space—are degraded in a moment into a set of villagers."

Some of the brighter asteroids have been used for determining the sun's parallax and distance from the earth, and with considerable success.

JUPITER.

JUPITER, FEBRUARY 12, 1888 (W.F.D.).
18h. 35m. (10-inch Reflector.)

VII.

JUPITER.

This giant planet, the largest member of the solar system, revolves round the sun in a period of nearly twelve of our years at a mean distance of about 476 millions of miles. The equatorial diameter is about 86,000 miles, nearly eleven times that of the earth. In volume therefore it exceeds the earth over 1,200 times, and it exceeds in bulk all the other planets of the Solar System put together! Its mass, however, owing to its smaller specific gravity, is only about 300 times greater than the mass of the earth.[1] The most ancient mention of this planet is an approach to the star δ Cancri, B.C., 240, September 3, recorded by Ptolemy. The planet is sensibly flattened at the north and south poles, the ratio of the equatorial to the polar diameter being about 106 to 100.[1] This degree of compression agrees with calculations founded on a consideration of its great rapidity of rotation—a rotation performed in the wonderfully

[1] See Appendix, Note E.

short period—for so large a planet—of 9 hours, 55 minutes, 35 seconds, according to Marth, and 9 hours, 55 minutes, 37 seconds, according to Denning, which is therefore the length of its day. Denning, however, considers that the true period of rotation may be even shorter than this. The brilliancy of Jupiter is so great that it has been seen with the naked eye in bright sunshine by Bond in America, and Denning in England; and Tebbutt finds it visible in full daylight at those oppositions which occur near the perihelion. It is a splendid telescopic object, and the phenomena of its belts and satellites form an interesting study. The belts were discovered by Zucchi at Rome in 1630, and generally lie nearly parallel to the equator of the planet. They are not constant features, however, but are subject to remarkable changes. Occasionally perfectly round bright spots similar to satellites in transit are visible in the southern hemisphere of the planet, and Sir John Herschel considered that possibly these luminous spots may be insulated masses of cloud similar to cumuli in the earth's atmosphere. The well-known painter, Mr. John Brett, has observed shadows cast by some of the white patches near the equator of Jupiter which seem to show that these spots are elevated above the general surface of the planet. The eminent observer, Ranyard, has shown that spots on Jupiter are more prevalent when spots on the sun are most numerous, and

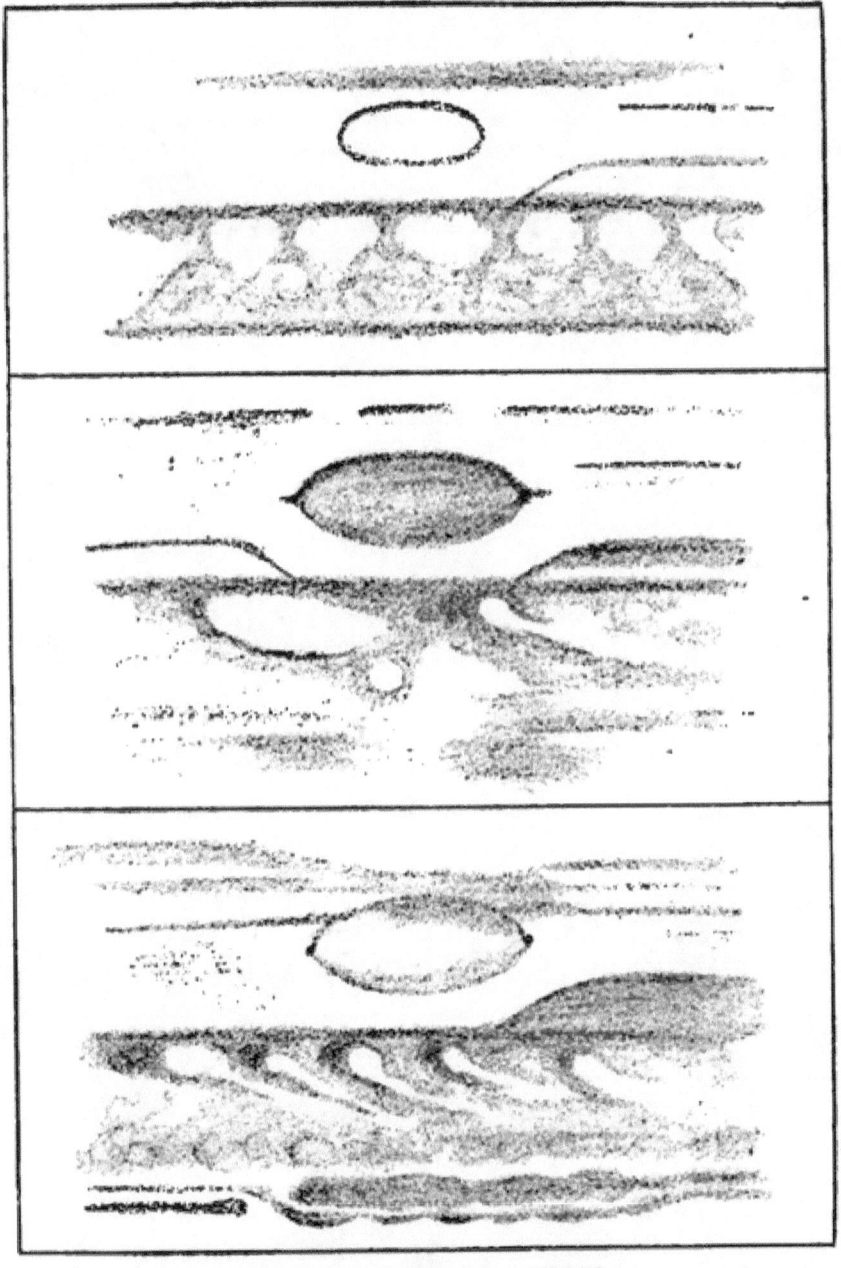

THE MARKINGS ON JUPITER.

1. Gledhill's Ellipse. 1870, Jan. 23, 8h. 20m.
2. Red Spot and region near. 1882, Oct. 30, 15h. 40m. (W. F. D.)
3. Red Spot and region near. 1886, Oct. 11, 11h. 54m. (W. F. D.)

thinks that possibly both phenomena may be due to the same cosmical cause. This idea is confirmed by Browning, who finds that the red colour of the belts coincides with the epoch of sun-spot maxima. A very remarkable reddish spot has been visible in recent years. It consists of an elliptical marking lying apparently on the surface of the planet, near the great southern belt. The longer axis of this ellipse measures about 25,000 miles in length, and the shorter axis about 6,500 miles. This wonderful object, after remaining visible for several years, almost totally disappeared about the end of August, 1883. In 1884 it was very faint and difficult to be seen, but it afterwards partly reappeared, and in 1885 was observed to have its central position apparently covered with a white cloud, thus giving it the appearance of an elliptical ring. It subsequently, however, became more prominent, and recent observations show that, although faint when compared with its appearance in 1880-81, it is more distinct than it was in 1884. From observations by Denning it seems that the position of this great red spot on the surface of Jupiter was not fixed, but had a motion of its own relative to other markings on the planet; and this excellent observer thinks that the spot is probably identical with one observed by Gledhill and Meyer in 1869-71.

The spectrum of Jupiter, according to Vogel, differs from that of the sun by the presence of some dark bands, the most remarkable of these being a dark band in the red, and from these bands he infers the existence of watery vapour in the planet's atmosphere. Situated as it is at such an immense distance from the sun, the great brightness of Jupiter seems scarcely explicable except on the supposition that it possesses some inherent light of its own; and some astronomers consider that the planet is actually in a red-hot state, and in fact plays the part of a miniature sun to its attendant family of planets. Its small density—less than one-fourth that of the earth—seems also in favour of of this hypothesis. An observation by Mr. Todd, of the Adelaide Observatory, Australia, in which he saw one of the satellites shining through the edge of the disc, would seem to indicate that the planet's atmosphere is several thousand miles in thickness!

Jupiter is attended by four satellites or moons, which are visible with any small telescope; one or two of them have even been seen with the naked eye by persons gifted with very sharp eyesight. They were discovered by Galileo in January, 1610. They are usually distinguished by numbers, the innermost being known as I., and the outermost as IV. No II. is about the size of our moon, and the others larger, No. III. being in size between Mercury and Mars. With a good telescope their transits across the disc of Jupiter, their occultations behind the disc, and their eclipses in the shadow

JUPITER, FEB. 3, 1882, 7h. 5m.
T. GWYN ELGER.
8½in. Calver-Reflector, Power 284.
Red Spot coming on Disc.

of the planet, form very interesting phenomena. Schröter found that the rotation of the satellites take place—like our own moon—in a period equal to that of its revolution round the planet, and that this law is common to the four satellites. Pickering considers that Satellite IV. is variable in light. Sir J. Herschel thought that perhaps an additional satellite—similar to Saturn's satellite, Japetus, and our own moon—might be worth searching for, but this now seems more than doubtful. Spots have been seen on the disc of III., and during transit this satellite is often seen quite as black as the shadow it casts on the face of the planet! On one occasion the American astronomer Bond saw III. on the disc of Jupiter as a black spot lying between its own shadow and the shadow of I., and not to be distinguished from either shadow except by its position. Dark transits of I. and IV. have also been seen. These dark transits seemed to favour the theory of inherent light in the planet, but it has lately been shown by Dr. Spitta by experiments with models suitably arranged and illuminated that these perplexing phenomena are simply due to the differences in the relative albedos (relative brightness of surface) of the satellites as compared with that of Jupiter, "and is not dependent upon the relative quantity of light reflected by one on the other, or upon any physical peculiarities in the Jovian system." Some of the phenomena, however, recorded by excellent observers seem very difficult of explanation. For instance, Cassini once failed to see the shadow of No. I. when it should have been on the disc. Trouvelot, in April 24, 1877, saw the shadow of the same satellite double! and a similar observation was recorded by South many years ago. On one occasion, Satellite II. having passed on to the disc of the planet in the usual way when a transit is about to take place, was observed by the late Admiral Smyth (a famous observer) several minutes afterwards outside the disc, where it remained for some minutes, and then vanished altogether! This observation was confirmed by two other observers at different places. At Stoneyhurst in November, 1880, the shadow of I. was observed to be very faint, and that of III. very small. There exists a remarkable relation between the mean motions of the three interior satellites, from which it results that the three cannot all be eclipsed at the same time.[1]

The observations of Jupiter's satellites led to the discovery of the progressive motion of light. It was found that the eclipses of the satellites took place some 8 minutes earlier than the calculated time when Jupiter was on the same side of its orbit as the earth, and about 8 minutes later when on the opposite side. This difference was soon found to be due to the time occupied by light in passing across the diameter of the earth's orbit. The velocity of

[1] See Appendix, Note E.

light computed in this way has been fully confirmed by the independent experiments of Foucault and Fizeau. The latest determination of this velocity is 186,290 miles per second.

SATURN.

SATURN.
Rings seen Edgeways (p. 72).

VIII.

SATURN.

THIS wonderful planet, with its extraordinary system of luminous rings, is perhaps the most interesting, as it certainly is the most unique member of the Solar System. It revolves round the sun in a period of about $29\frac{1}{2}$ years, at a mean distance of about 872 millions of miles, or more than nine times the earth's distance from the sun. In size it is second only to Jupiter, having a diameter of about 72,000 miles, or about nine times that of the earth. In density, however, it is extremely light [1] (specific gravity = 0·68), so light, indeed, that it would float in water like a ball of wood, and the existence of a heavy liquid like water on its surface is therefore improbable. The flattening at the poles is greater than that of any other planet, the ellipticity being, according to Meyer $\frac{1}{11.5}$, and according to Kaiser about $\frac{1}{9}$. The period of rotation on its axis is 10 hours, 14 minutes, 24 seconds, according to Prof. Hall. The equator of

[1] See Appendix, Note F.

the planet is inclined to the ecliptic at an angle of about 28 degrees, or very similar to that of the earth. Athough the brightness of the planet is not very great—about half that of Vega according to Seidel—there seems to be some reason for supposing that possibly it possesses some inherent light of its own, due perhaps to its being in a red-hot state like Jupiter.

Belts and spots have been observed on its surface similar to those of Jupiter, but not so clearly defined, owing to its greater distance from the earth.

Saturn is attended by eight satellites, which have been named (commencing with the nearest to the planet), Mimas, Enceladus, Tethys, Dione, Rhea, Titan, Hyperion, and Japetus. The largest of these, Titan, may be seen with any small telescope, and is probably in size about equal to Mercury, or about 3000 miles in diameter. The two innermost, Mimas and Enceladus, are very faint, and can only be seen in large telescopes. Hyperion is also faint, and is probably less than 1000 miles in diameter. The remaining five satellites may perhaps be seen with a good telescope of 4-inch aperture under favourable circumstances.

The inner satellite, Mimas, revolves round Saturn in a period of 22 hours 37 minutes. Titan takes 15 days, 22 hours, and 41 minutes, and the outermost Japetus, 79 days, 7 hours, and 49 minutes. The light of Japetus is variable, due probably to rotation on its axis, which seems to be performed in the same time as its revolution round the planet, as in the case of our own moon, and, according to Schröter, this is also true for Tethys, Dione, Rhea, and Titan. According to Hall, the five inner satellites move in the plane of the ring, and in orbits which are sensibly circular.

The system of rings is without a parallel among celestial bodies. That they cannot possibly be solid has been fully proved by mathematicians on mechanical principles. A liquid or gaseous composition is also out of the question, and the only theory which will bear the test of mathematical analysis is that they consist of a swarm of very small satellites revolving round the planet in separate orbits, somewhat similar to the zone of minor planets which revolve round the sun between Mars and Jupiter. The ring system consists of 3 separate rings, the outer one, which measures about 166,000 miles in diameter, being somewhat fainter than the centre ring, from which it is separated by a dark division, discovered by Cassini in 1675. This division is visible in a telescope of very moderate size. The inner ring, known as the "gauze" or "crape" ring, is very much darker than the others, and is usually described by observers as of a purple or slaty hue. It was only discovered in the year 1850 (independently by Bond, in America, and Dawes, in

England), although the planet was in previous years carefully examined by the Herschels and other celebrated observers. How it escaped the notice of Sir W. Herschel with his great reflector is difficult to understand, and it has been even suggested that it has probably become brighter in recent years. Some observers have suspected a division in this dark ring. Another division was seen by Encke in the outer ring, but later observations seems to show that this division is not a constant feature, as it is sometimes seen in small telescopes, and at others is quite invisible even in large instruments. Supposing the dark ring to consist, like the other rings, of a swarm of small satellites, these must be much less numerous, as the ring is semi-transparent, the ball of the planet being visible through the ring! Owing to the inclined position of the rings, and the change in the relative position of the earth, and Saturn caused by their revolution round the sun, the ring system is in some years more open than in others. The rings were most open in the years 1885-6. They are now closing again, and will continue to do so till the years 1891-2, when they will be presented edgeways to the earth, and become invisible, except in the largest telescopes, the thickness of the rings probably not exceeding 100 miles.

The shadow of the planet on the rings can be easily seen with a small telescope; anything much over 2 inches in aperture will generally show it well.

The American mathematician Kirkwood has shown that the divisions in the rings are due to the disturbance caused by the attraction of the satellites on the materials composing the rings. He shows that these gaps are analogous to those observed in the zone of asteroids between Mars and Jupiter, and that on this theory there *should* be a division in the outer ring, somewhat nearer to the outer than the inner edge of the ring. The position of Cassini's division also agrees with this theory, which now seems to be in perfect accordance with observation.

An observation by the eminent English observer, Captain Noble, seems to show that the ball of the planet is not concentric with the ring system, the centre of the ball being sensibly south of the plane of the rings.

As Webb says "to a spectator placed on Mimas, revolving in less than 23 hours, at a distance of only 32,000 miles from the edge of the outer ring, the whole system of rings and the included globe would float before the eye in such a spectacle of grandeur and beauty as the imagination is wholly unequal to conceive."

In the ancient Chaldean mythology, the planet Saturn was associated with the great triune deity Nisroch or Asshur, and it is a curious fact that, in the Assyrian sculptures, this god is represented by the figure of a man encircled by a ring. This was of course long before the invention of the telescope, and has led to the idea, that considering the changes probably now in progress in the ring system, it may possibly have had considerably larger dimensions four thousand years ago, and might then probably have been just visible to the keen-sighted vision of the old Chaldean astronomers.

Müller finds that the light of Saturn, when the earth is at an elevation of 26 degrees above the plane of the rings, is 2·4 times greater than when the earth is in that plane, or, in other words, the brightness of the rings in the former position is 58·3 per cent. of the brightness of the whole Saturnian system.

URANUS.

IX.

URANUS.

This planet was discovered by Sir William Herschel, on March 13, 1781, while engaged in examining some small stars in Gemini. He at first supposed it to be a comet, and, indeed, announced it as such to the Royal Society, on April 26th. On the calculation of its orbit, however, it was soon found to be a planet, exterior to Saturn, and revolving round the sun in a period of over 84 years, at a mean distance of about 1754 millions of miles, or nearly 19 times the distance of the earth from the sun. An inspection of earlier observations shows that Uranus had previously been observed no less than 20 times, and mistaken for a fixed star. It was observed by Flamsteed so early as 1690, and registered as a star. In Lalande's Catalogue (published by the British Association), the planet is entered as No. 20,592. This supposed star was missed at Markree Observatory some years ago, and now proves to have been the planet. These earlier observations have been found very useful in determining the elements of the planet's orbit. The diameter of the planet is about 33,000 miles, or about 72 times larger than the earth in volume. In density, however, it is only about equal in weight to water, so that its mass is only about $12\frac{1}{2}$ times greater than that of the earth.[1] The inclination of the orbit to the plane of the ecliptic is only 0° $46\frac{1}{2}'$, or less than that of any of the other large planets. Schiaparelli finds a flattening at the poles of about $\frac{1}{12}$, and Young $\frac{1}{14}$, or greater than any other planet with exception of Saturn. Flammarion thinks the period of rotation may be about 10 hours, 40 minutes, but this is doubtful owing to the difficulty of observing any spots on its small disc.

Uranus is attended by four satellites; the two outer, Titania (3) and Oberon (4), were discovered by Sir W. Herschel in 1787, and the two inner, Ariel (1) and Umbriel (2), by Lassell in 1847. They revolve round the planet in periods, varying from $2\frac{1}{2}$ to $13\frac{1}{2}$ days, in orbits inclined at the high (and very unusual) inclination of about 79 degrees to the plane of the planet's orbit. These faint satellites are only visible in large telescopes, and little or nothing is known about their size or physical condition.

Uranus may just be seen with the naked eye when its position in the heavens is accurately known. Zöllner found the mean stellar magnitude to be

[1] See Appendix, Note G.

5·46. On March 12, 1880, when the planet was near Rho Leonis, I estimated it as brighter than 49 Leonis, but fainter than 48 Leonis. Taking the Harvard photometric measures of these stars, this observation would make the apparent magnitude of Uranus on that date as about 5·5. On May 21, 1886, I found Uranus equal in brightness to 7 Virginis, and brighter than 10 and 13 Virginis, or about 5·3 magnitude. The planet was on that date a little south of the bright star Eta Virginis.

Examined with the spectroscope, Huggins and Secchi find the spectum of Uranus an extraordinary one, showing six absorption bands.

NEPTUNE.

PATH OF NEPTUNE.

X.

NEPTUNE.

The discovery of this planet—the outermost member of the Solar System as far as is yet known—was one of the greatest triumphs of astronomical and mathematical science. For many years after the discovery of Uranus it was found impossible to reconcile the observations with the earlier positions of the planet, when it was observed as a fixed star. These irregularities in the motion of Uranus at last became so great that astronomers were led to suspect that they were really due to the disturbing action of an exterior planet, and the enormously difficult problem of calculating the place of the unknown planet was attacked in 1844-45 by two young mathematicians, Adams in England, and Le Verrier in France. In October, 1845, Adams, and in June, 1846, Le Verrier, arrived independently at nearly the same results. Unfortunately, however, Adams' results were not published at the time. On the publication of Le Verrier's result in 1846, a search for the planet was instituted at Cambridge Observatory by Challis, but owing to the want of suitable star charts the work proceeded slowly, and the planet was not identified, although it had been actually observed as a star on two nights. Meanwhile the planet was discovered by Galle at Berlin, with the aid of Bremiker's star charts, on Sept. 23, 1846, in a position between those pointed out by Adams and Le Verrier, but nearer to the place given by the French astronomer.

Neptune was observed as a fixed star twice by Lalande, viz., on May 8 and 10, 1795, and it is entered as No. 26,266 ($7\frac{1}{2}$ magnitude) in the reduced Catalogue, published by the British Association. In the notes to the Catalogue, Baily says, "The star observed by Lalande on May 10, 1795, is undoubtedly the planet (*Neptune*). On consulting the original MSS. it appears that he observed the planet on May 10, 1795, *and also on* May 8, 1795; but in printing the 'Histoire Céleste,' these two observations, supposed to be the same fixed star, were found discordant: hence the observation of May 8 *was not printed at all*, and to that of May 10 were affixed the two points, signifying doubt, which are not in the MSS." Here we have another important discovery missed by rejecting an *apparently* faulty observation, but which was nevertheless probably correct. The planet is entered in Harding's Atlas as an 8-mag. star (about $1\frac{1}{2}$ degrees north following λ Virginis), probably on the authority of Lalande's observation

Neptune was also observed and recorded as a fixed star by Lamont, October 25, 1845, and Sept. 7 and 11, 1846.

Neptune revolves round the sun in a period of about 164½ years, at a mean distance of about 2,746 millions of miles, or about thirty times the earth's mean distance from the sun. The eccentricity of the orbit is smaller than that of any of the other large planets, with the exception of Venus. The diameter of the planet is about 36,000 miles, or a little greater than that of Uranus. Its density (0·96) is about the same as that of Uranus. (See Appendix, note H.)

Little or nothing is known about the physical condition of this remote planet, as owing to its great distance from the earth it is not possible to observe any markings on its surface, even with the largest telescopes. Flammarion thinks the period of rotation is about 10 hours 58 minutes, but this is of course very doubtful.

Neptune is attended by only one satellite, discovered by Lassell in 1846. It revolves round the planet in a period of about 5 days 21 hours, at a mean distance of about 220,000 miles. The fact of its being visible at all at such a distance leads to the belief that it is probably the largest satellite in the Solar System, but nothing further is known about its actual size or physical condition. The orbit is inclined to the ecliptic at an angle of about 35°, according to Newcomb, and, like the satellites of Uranus, its motion is retrograde. There seems to be some suspicion that there may possibly exist a second satellite, fainter than the known one and very difficult to be seen.

DOUBLE STARS.

XI.

DOUBLE STARS.[1]

A LARGE number of the stars have been found to be telescopically double, and considering the number of these objects whose components are so close as to require our most powerful telescopes to show them as anything but single stars, it appears probable that the real number of the double stars is much greater than those actually discovered. Mr. Burnham's numerous discoveries in recent years of doubles hitherto undetected—and with a telescope of very moderate aperture (six inches) compared with the giant instruments now mounted in the principal observatories—render it probable that with an increase of optical power the list of doubles may be considerably increased.

The double stars have been divided into two classes, those merely optically double, and binaries, or those which are physically connected by the laws of gravitation. The components of a binary are, as

[1] "English Mechanic," 1872.

a rule, very close, and consequently require considerable telescopic power to divide them. There are, however, notable exceptions to this rule—for instance, a Centauri, Castor, and others.

In cases where the interval is considerable, as in β Cygni and δ Orionis, it is highly probable that the component stars are merely accidentally close together, the real distance separating one from the other being possibly, in some cases, as great as that which divides the nearest from the earth. The probability, however, of such an accidental arrangement occurring in a large number of cases is so small as to lead us to the belief that in the majority of doubles there is a physical connection existing between the stars. The apparent distance separating them would, to a great extent, depend on their distance from the earth. Thus in a Centauri and 61 Cygni we have examples of wide binaries, the interval being considerable owing to their relative proximity to our system. Close binaries are probably at a much greater distance, except in those doubles—like 58 Pegasi—in which the companion to a tolerably bright star is very faint, in which case the small "star" may not improbably be a very large planet, perhaps possessing, like Jupiter, considerable intrinsic brilliancy, but having a much greater diameter in proportion to its primary sun than Mr. Proctor's "giant planet."

Our own sun is evidently *not* a double star, no star

in the heavens being sufficiently near him to be considered as a companion.

There are also known a number of triple stars, forming still more interesting combinations. Several of these have been found from careful observations to have—like the double stars—a physical connection. Others are quadruple and even multiple, and some of these also are suspected of forming systems connected by gravitation.

The orbits of a number of the binary stars have been calculated by various astronomers, and found to be in every case elliptical, with periods varying from about 11 years to over 1,600. M. Savary was the first to compute a binary star orbit, viz., that of ξ Ursæ Majoris, for which he found a period of about 58 years. Later computations of this remarkable binary make the period about 61 years. The period of revolution of the components of Castor has been variously computed at periods ranging from 232 years (Mädler, 1842) to 1,001 years (Doberck). The latter period is now considered to be the most correct. The period of γ Virginis is about 185 years (Thiele), and that of ζ Aquarii, according to Doberck, about 1,625 years.[1] The star Zeta Herculis is another remarkable binary. Its period is about $34\frac{1}{2}$ years, and it has on three occasions been observed as a single star, viz., by Sir W. Herschel in 1802, by Struve from 1828 to 1831, and by Secchi in

[1] See Appendix, Note I.

1865, thus exhibiting the rare phenomenon of one star occulted by another!

If these binary stars have planets revolving round them, their motions, owing to the mutual perturbations, must be very complicated. If each star has its own system of planets, they must be, in most cases, nearer to the central sun than Neptune is in our system, otherwise the outermost planets in each system would greatly interfere with each others motion. It seems more probable, however, that the attendant planets perform their revolutions round the common centre of gravity of both suns, and thus the inhabitants (if any there be) of these distant worlds must at intervals enjoy the spectacle of two suns above their horizon at the same time, probably of different colours, except in the case of those possessing complimentary colours, the combined effect producing white light when both suns are above the horizon.

VARIABLE STARS.

XII.

VARIABLE STARS.

A number of the stars have been found to be variable in their light. A few have been known for a great number of years, and their variations carefully watched. One of the most remarkable of these interesting and mysterious objects is *o* Ceti, termed *Mira*, or the wonderful, which was first observed in 1596 by Fabricius. Its mean period from maximum to maximum is about 331 days, but this varies to some extent. The light varies from about the 2nd magnitude to the 9th, but its brightness at maximum is very variable. At the maximum of 1799 it was thought by Sir W. Herschel to be but little inferior to Aldebaran, while at the maximum of 1868 it did not exceed the 5th magnitude! In several books on astronomy it is stated that Mira was invisible at the epoch of maxima during the years 1672 to 1676, but this is a mistake, as it was long since (in 1837) pointed out by Bianchi that the supposed invisibility of Mira in those years was simply due to the fact that the maxima occurred at a time of year when the star was near the sun and could not be observed. The same thing seems to have happened in the years 1852, 1853, 1854, and 1883. The star was very favourably placed for observation in the years 1885 to 1887, but did not in the last three maxima rise above the 4th magnitude. The variability of Algol (β Persei) was first noticed by Montanari in 1667 or 1669, and after him by Miraldi, Kirch, and Palitzsch, but the true character of its variation was first determined by Goodricke in 1782. It goes through all its changes in 2 days, 20 hours, 48 minutes, 51 seconds; and for the greater portion of its period the light is constant at about 2nd magnitude. It then begins to diminish, and in about $4\frac{1}{2}$ hours is reduced to nearly the 4th magnitude. It remains at the minimum for about 15 or 20 minutes, and then gradually regains its normal brightness, the whole of the light changes taking place in a period of about 10 hours.[1]

There are other short period variables, such as δ Cephei, β Lyræ, η Aquilæ, 10 Sagittæ, whose light is constantly varying within small limits in a period of a few days. Others, like μ Cephei, vary in an irregular manner, and have no fixed period.

Several theories have been proposed to account for the curious, and in many cases very capricious and irregular, variations exhibited by these interest-

[1] See Appendix, Note J.

ing objects. Some writers have suggested that they are surrounded by an atmosphere irregular in its density, but this theory does not appear a satisfactory one. A more probable explanation has been advanced, namely, that these suns—for suns they probably are—are subject to periodical outbursts of sun spots, which occasionally increase so much, both in number and magnitude, as to appreciably diminish their light. This appears a very probable theory— at least as far as the long period and irregular variables are concerned—when we consider the extent to which our own sun is occasionally—at the maximum of the "sun spot period"—covered by these curious blots, and which have at several periods in history increased to an extraordinary extent, so much so that at one time the sun is said to have lost half its light. This is probably an exaggeration, but still it is possible that the number of spots visible at these times may have exceeded considerably those visible of late years. This theory would satisfactorily account for those variables like β Orionis (Betelgeuse), in which the periods are long, and the variations small and irregular. But for those having short and regular periods we must look for some other explanation as a *vera causa*. For variables of the Algol type the most probable appears to be the following. Suppose the sun in question to be attended by an immensely large planet, whose size bears a much greater proportion to the primary than Jupiter does to the sun, and suppose it to have—unlike Jupiter—little or no reflecting power or intrinsic light, it would, though quite invisible in the most powerful telescopes, cut off a considerable portion of the star's light when transiting the disc of its primary. The variations in brilliancy would of course depend on the magnitude of the dark satellite which, if nearly approaching in diameter the central sun, might cut off a large portion of the light. This theory has lately been ably advocated by Professor Pickering.[1]

A more probable explanation of the variation in stars like δ Cephei, η Aquilæ, &c., is that these variables revolve, like our own sun, upon their axis in a fixed period, and that a portion of their surface is from some cause—whether from a large number of permanent spots or otherwise—very much less luminous than the rest, and consequently when this darker portion is turned towards the earth there is a corresponding diminution in the light of the star.

With regard to those still more extraordinary objects known as temporary or "new" stars, which have at intervals in history burst forth with a brilliancy exceeding in some cases that of the brightest stars in the heavens, and which have attracted the attention of the most superficial observers, it is more difficult to suggest any satisfactory explanation. Some have considered them merely

[1] See Appendix, Note J.

as variables with immensely long periods. The great length of the period, however, which must necessarily be assumed, renders the truth of this supposition extremely doubtful. The most probable theory appears to be that the immense increase in their light is due to the heat caused by collision with some dark body, or cloud of meteors, giving rise to an outburst of hydrogen gas, as was shown by Dr. Huggins to have taken place in the star in Corona Borealis, which suddenly blazed out in May, 1866. Similar eruptions, though of course on a small scale, have been observed in the sun by Professor Young and other observers with the aid of the spectroscope, and the immense "prominences" which are seen surrounding the sun during a total eclipse are due to the same cause. In the case of the star in Corona the great increase of light may possibly have been caused by the conflagration of one of its attendant planets, as we are led by Scripture to believe that our own earth will one day be consumed, and that its "elements will melt with fervent heat," doubtless giving off, with other gases, the incandescent hydrogen detected by Dr. Huggins in the light of the "Blaze star."

Among the more remarkable of the long-period variables may be mentioned the following—in addition to Mira Ceti, already described.

χ Cygni. This very remarkable variable was discovered by G. Kirch so far back as the year 1686.

The mean period is about 406½ days, but according to Schönfeld the observations cannot be represented by a uniform period, as the mean period gives the maxima in the years 1687 to 1738, and since 1863 too early; and in 1747-1758, and 1821-1862 too late; but on the whole the observations show a small lengthening of the period. From the observations of recent years the minimum light, which Schönfeld gives at 12·8 magnitude, seems to occur about 185 days before the maximum. The light at maximum varies from 4 mag. to 6 mag., but the star rarely reaches the 4th magnitude. At some maxima the star is barely visible to the naked eye. Thus at the maximum of 1882, Sept. 1, Schmidt estimated it only 6·1 mag. I observed maxima, 1883, Oct. 19 (4·9 mag.); 1884, Nov. 23 (4·65 mag.); and 1886, Jan. 6 ±. There are numerous small stars in the immediate vicinity of the variable. The variable is Bayer's χ Cygni, and has been frequently confused with 17 (Flamsteed) Cygni, to which Flamsteed affixed the letter χ by mistake; the variable, which is the true χ having been faint at the date of Flamsteed's observation. It has been proposed to call 17 χ, and the variable χ^2, but there is nothing to be gained by perpetuating an error of this sort. The variable is very reddish in colour, and shows in the spectroscope a magnificent spectrum of Secchi's third type.

R Leonis. A remarkable variable discovered by Koch in 1782. From a discussion of the observations since the year 1818, Schönfeld deduces a mean period of $312\frac{1}{2}$ days. There are some irregularities at both maxima and minima, but no general lengthening or shortening of the period seems to have taken place since the days of Bradley and T. Mayer. At maximum the magnitude varies from 5·2 to 7·0, and at mimimum from 9 to 10 mag. At the maximum of 1877, March 6, which I observed in Northern India, the star was about 5·2 mag., being then slightly brighter than ν Leonis. At the maximum of 1878, Jan. 18, Schwab found it only 7 mag. At the maximum of 1883, March 19, I estimated it $5\frac{1}{2}$ mag.— slightly less than ν Leonis; and at the maximum of 1884, Jan. 27, I found it only $6\frac{1}{2}$ mag. A minimum of 9 mag was observed by Schmidt, 1882, Nov. 9. It lies closely south of 19 (Flamsteed) Leonis, with which star it has been sometimes confused. Closely preceding it are two small stars which form with the variable an isosceles triangle. It is red in all phases of its light, and Hind says, "It is one of the most fiery-looking variables on our list—fiery in every stage from maximum to minimum, and is really a fine telescopic object in a dark sky, about the time of greatest brilliancy, when its colour forms a striking contrast with the steady white light of the 6 mag. a little to the north." Its spectrum is a splendid one of Secchi's third type. Dunér says, "Le spectre est aussi beau que celui de Mira à la même grandeur," and d'Arrest describes its colour and spectrum as "Auffälig roth. Das spectrum gehört zum III. Typus mit breiten scharf gezeichten Zonen."

R (*v*) Hydræ. This remarkable variable star was first observed by Hevelius in April, 1662, but the character of its variations was first determined by Maraldi in 1704. It varies at the maximum from 4 to $5\frac{1}{2}$ magnitude, and at the minimum descends to the 10th magnitude. The period has, according to Schönfeld, diminished since the date of its discovery, having been about 500 days in 1708, 487 days in 1785, 461 days in 1825, and 437 days in 1870, and it seems to be still decreasing. Dr. Gould, at Cordoba, has studied the changes of this variable, and finds that the period is rapidly diminishing, the diminution amounting to about 9 hours in each period, and that there is a symmetric perturbation which completes its cycle in 72 years. Heis gives the minimum as 11 mag., and according to Schmidt the minimum precedes the maximum by about 200 days. I observed maxima of this star, 1875, Feb. 10; 1876, April 12; and 1883, May 12 to 16. The star is very red, and the spectrum is a splendid example of Secchi's third type. Dunér describes it as "d'une beauté tout à fait extraordinaire. Il n'y a que le spectre de *o* Ceti qui l'égale;" the bands being extremely large and perfectly black: and Secchi says, "3° tipo superbo; risolubile ad intervalli. Nel giallo le zone sono poco separate. Dal magnesio al rosso sono poco distinte le zone. Alcune righe sono vivissime."

For a classification of the variable stars, see Appendix.

NEBULÆ.

XIII.

NEBULÆ.

WHEN the heavens are carefully examined with powerful telescopes we find that, in addition to the myriads of faint stars brought into view by their aid, there exist a large number of dim cometary-looking objects more or less thickly scattered in different portions of the sky. These are termed nebulæ, and the number now known to exist exceeds the number of stars visible to the naked eye in both hemispheres. Most of these objects can only be seen with a telescope. A few, however, can just be detected by the unassisted eyesight on a clear moonless night, if their position is accurately known. Of these may be mentioned the "great nebula in Andromeda," first alluded to by Al-Sufi in the tenth century. It was described by Simon Marius in 1612, as resembling "a candle shining through a horn," which is not an inapt description of its appearance, as seen in an opera glass. Its general form is that of a long oval, or elongated ellipse, considerably brighter towards the centre. Examined with powerful telescopes its aspect is much altered, and two dark longitudinal streaks become apparent which are not visible in smaller instruments. Though even with high powers the nebulæ remains, as a whole, nebulous, still numerous small stars appear thickly scattered over it, and seem to lead to the belief that with more powerful optical aid the nebulous portion would be completely resolvable into stars. In the spectroscope it gives a continuous spectrum, which shows that whatever may be its nature, it is not gaseous. A temporary star suddenly made its appearance near the nucleus of this nebula, in August, 1885, and further details are given on another page.[1] Many of the nebulæ are easily resolvable into stars with powerful telescopes. For instance, the nebulæ in Hercules (13 Messier), and ω Centauri. Others are quite irresolvable, and remain hazy in appearance under the highest powers which can be applied to the largest and most perfect telescopes. A number of these have been found by Dr. Huggins, from observations with the spectroscope, to consist of glowing gas, chiefly hydrogen and nitrogen. Their nature is probably that of a vast mass of incandescent gas undergoing a process of cooling and condensation. Many of the nebulæ exhibit tolerably well-defined outlines, particularly those called "planetary" nebulæ. Others show very irregular shapes, and

[1] See page 157.

present an appearance somewhat similar to that of a light fleecy cloud wafted about by the wind. These are generally the largest, that is, cover the greatest apparent area in the heavens. Of these large and irregular nebulæ, the most remarkable visible in these latitudes is that in the "sword" of Orion surrounding the multiple star θ Orionis, the four brighter stars of which compose the well-known "trapezium" of telescopists. This nebulæ is of considerable extent, covering a space in the heavens larger than the full moon. It is just perceptible to the naked eye of a clear night as a patch of hazy light. It was carefully observed by Sir J. Herschel with his large telescope at the Cape of Good Hope, and described by him as "offering a resemblance to the head and yawning jaws of some monstrous animal, with a sort of proboscis running out from the snout." Even with the high powers applied by Herschel to his large instruments, its light still remained nebulous and irresolvable. It was at one time considered by Lord Rosse to show symptoms of resolutions into stars when viewed through his giant reflector, with high powers and under favourable circumstances. Later observations, however, by Huggins, with the spectroscope, prove that it consists of nothing but glowing gas, probably hydrogen and nitrogen. Dr. Huggins remarks, "The light from the brightest parts of the nebulæ near the trapezium was resolved by the prisms into three bright lines in all respects similar to those of the gaseous nebulæ. The whole of this great nebula as far as lies within the power of my instrument emits light which is identical in its character. The light from one part differs from the light of another in intensity alone." Thus the "nebular hypothesis" which Herschel considered to have received such strong support from the discovery of so many nebulous objects, but which was thought to have received its death blow when Lord Rosse's great telescope apparently resolved into stars numbers of nebulous objects, now gains fresh evidence in its favour from the results of spectroscopic research. Of some 70 nebulæ examined by Dr. Huggins, one third were found to give a gaseous spectrum, the light of the remainder—some of which are shown as clusters in the telescope—give stellar spectra. As the number of these objects which have been thus examined, is very small compared to the total number which have been discovered, we may conclude that the actual number of these masses of glowing gas is very considerable.

Those wonderful objects known as spiral nebulæ, discovered by the late Lord Rosse, would appear to afford further evidence of the correctness of the nebular theory when applied to the formation of clusters of stars. In these nebulæ it is very evident to the eye that the mass is rotating, and in one remarkable instance the 51st of Messier's Catalogue —a small round nebula is apparently attached to the end of the spiral, and looks as if it were on the point of parting from the parent mass by the force of the rotation.

It is not a little remarkable that all the gaseous nebulæ hitherto examined have been found to consist chiefly of hydrogen and nitrogen gases, which would of course last longer in the gaseous state than nebulæ consisting of the vapours of other elements, hydrogen and nitrogen requiring an immense degree of pressure and very intense cold to reduce them to the liquid or solid state.

Among the "planetary" nebulæ, the circular form generally predominates. They are so called from their resemblance to the discs shown by the planets; very much fainter of course, as none of them are visible without a telescope. This leads us to the conclusion that they cannot be composed of masses of stars, as, were they so, their intrinsic brightness would probably be much greater than it actually is. The largest object of this class is situated a little south of Beta Ursæ Majoris, the southern stars of the two "pointers." It subtends an angle of 2' 40", which, supposing it situated at the distance of the nearest fixed star, implies an actual diameter of about 200 times the sun's distance from the earth! Another remarkable object of this kind is visible near Delta Geminorum, and south of Pollux. It has a small star—perfectly stellar—in the centre. Lord Rosse described it as "a most astonishing object." Supposing this small star to be in reality physically connected with the nebula, and not merely optically superposed upon it, we have here further evidence in favour of the nebular hypothesis, which supposes that all suns and planets were originally formed by the condensation of nebulous matter.

Nebulæ easily resolvable into stars are called clusters, and of these the "globular" clusters are the most remarkable. One of the finest objects of this class is that situated between Eta and Zeta Herculis. It was discovered by Halley, in 1714, and may be just detected on a dark night by the unassisted eye. Sir W. Herschel estimated the number of stars it contains at 14,000! Another remarkable example is ω Centauri, in the southern hemisphere. It shines as a star of the 4th magnitude, and to the naked eye very much resembles a small comet without a tail. Examined with a powerful telescope, however, it is seen to be composed of an immense multitude of stars of about the 15th magnitude, very much condensed towards the centre, which is just the appearance a globular mass of stars would present when viewed at a distance. The cluster known as 47 Toucani presents a similar aspect. The beauty and magnificence of the spectacle afforded by these globular clusters, when viewed with powerful instruments, is such as cannot be adequately described, and it has been said that when seen for the first time in a large telescope, few "can refrain from a sort of rapture." The component stars, though distinctly visible as points of light, defy all attempts at counting them, and seem literally innumerable. Placed like a mass of glittering diamond dust on the dark background of the heavens, they impress us forcibly with the idea that if each of these points of light is a sun the thousands which appear massed together in so small a space, must be in reality either relatively close, and individually small, or else the system of suns must be placed at a distance almost approaching the infinite.

Mr. Proctor's interesting researches on the distribution of the nebulæ shows that the " zone of few nebulæ," as he terms it, coincides exactly with the Milky Way, in which the stars are most densely crowded. The nebulæ which do occur in the Milky Way are for the most part clusters, or easily resolvable nebulæ, thus suggesting the idea that the stars composing the Milky Way are merely nebulæ condensed into the solid state. The number of nebulæ which crowd the opposite region of the heavens would seem to be now undergoing the process of formation into stars, thus accounting in a satisfactory manner for the marked absence of stars in regions where nebulæ abound.

The following are some notes on nebulæ and clusters observed by the present writer in India :—

1. Dunlop 535 in Argo. R.A., 7h. 47m., S., 38° 1'

(1870). Described by Sir John Herschel as "Superb cluster, gradually brighter in the middle ; 20' diameter. Rich. Stars very remarkably equal. All 12 or 13 magnitude." I found the brighter stars well seen with a power of 133 on 3-inch refractor in 1875. A stream of larger stars runs from it in a northern direction, like the stem of a cornucopia.

2. Sir W. Herschel's VII., 12. R.A., 7h. 2m., S., 5° 24' (1870), in Canis Major. 3° east of γ and about 30' *following* a 6 mag. star. A good many stars of larger magnitudes, which seem fainter than 9 mag. A star about 8½ mag. with a small companion nearly *following*, 3-inch refractor, 1875.

3. Messier 8, in Sagittarius. R.A., 17h. 56m., S., 24° 21' (1870). *South following* 4 Sagittarii (4 mag.). The star 9 Sagittarii (7 mag.) is involved in the nebulæ "followed by a great cluster VI. 13 which with the nebula fills many fields" (Sir J. Herschel). Webb says, "visible to the naked eye." I found it plain to the naked eye in the Punjab. A glorious object even with 3 inches ; the cluster f being beautifully seen, but the nebula is milky looking, though several small stars are visible in it. The star 7 Sagittarii *preceding* is a very wide double, the companion being also double. The cluster lies midway between two 8 mag. stars.

4. Messier 22, in Sagittarius. R.A., 18h. 29m., S., 24° 1' (1880). Herschel says, "Globular ; very bright, large and compressed ; 7' diameter. The

stars are of two magnitudes, viz., 15-16 and 12 mag., and what is very remarkable, the largest of the latter are visibly reddish; one in particular, the largest of all *s.f.* the middle, is decidedly a ruddy star, and so I think are all the other large ones." About $2\frac{1}{2}°$ *north following* λ Sagittarii. Webb says the largest of the components are 10 and 11 mag. I found the larger star well seen with 133 on 3-inch refractor. They seem much fainter than 10 and 11. Herschel's estimate of 12 mag. is more correct. The greater portion of the cluster is nebulous with 3 inches.

5. Messier 55, in Sagittarius. R.A., 19h. 31m., S., 31° 16'. Sir J. Herschel says, "Globular; a fine, large, round cluster; all clearly resolved into stars 11, 12, 13 mag.; does not come up to a nipple." It lies 9° following ζ Sagittarii, and *north preceding* a 5 mag. star. I saw glimpses of stars in it with a power of 40 on 3 inches in 1875. It will not bear a higher power with this aperture; very much like, but not so bright as, the Hercules cluster (13 Messier). The larger stars seem fainter than 11 mag.

6. Dunlop 499. In Scorpio just north of $ζ^1$ and $ζ^2$. Very bright, visible to the naked eye in the Punjab, as a hazy star of 4 or $4\frac{1}{2}$ mag. The component stars well seen with 3 inches. A beautiful object for a small telescope.

7. About 4° north of λ Scorpii, is a beautiful cluster of stars, about 8th to 12th magnitudes, the stars arranged in particularly well-marked "streams," the

whole somewhat resembling in outline a bird's foot with three toes, the spaces enclosed by the stream being remarkably void of stars. This object is visible to the naked eye as a star of 5 or $5\frac{1}{2}$ magnitude.

8. In Scorpio R.A., 17h. 45m., S., 34° 47' (1870). Sir J. Herschel says, " A brilliant close cluster of about 60 stars, 7 to 12 mag., which fills the field." I found it visible to the naked eye in the Punjab sky. Beautifully seen with 3-inch refractor.

DISTANCES OF THE FIXED STARS.

XIV.

ON THE DISTANCES OF THE FIXED STARS.

To ascertain the distance of the stars from the earth was a problem which, until very lately, baffled all the powers of human ingenuity to solve. The distance of even the nearest is so immense that it is difficult to obtain a base line sufficiently long to form an appreciable triangle. In dealing with the distance of the sun, moon, and the principal planets of the Solar System, the earth's diameter was found sufficient, but when we come to estimate the distance of those minute points of light, which even in our largest telescopes, and with the highest magnifying powers, still remain as points, our base line is found to be totally inadequate for the purpose. We must then have recourse to the diameter of the earth's orbit round the sun as the base of our stellar triangle. Even with this immense line of about 186 millions of miles there are very few of the fixed stars which show any measurable displacement, or parallax, as it is called. Even with the nearest of them, which is supposed to be Alpha Centauri—a bright star in the Southern hemisphere—the parallax, or the angle subtended at the star by the semi-diameter of the earth's orbit, amounts to only about three-fourths of a single second of arc ($0'''75$)! Considerable difficulties exist in measuring so small an apparent change of place in a star's position, as numerous corrections have to be made on account of other apparent motions to which a star is liable, such as aberration, " proper motion," refraction, &c. These, combined with instrumental errors—from which not even the most perfect instruments are entirely free—render the investigation one of the utmost difficulty. These difficulties have, however, been successfully grappled with by several skilful observers and mathematicians, amongst whom may be mentioned Bessel, Henderson, Peters, and O. Struve, and in recent years, Sir R. S. Ball, Gill, Hall, and Pritchard. From observations of stars of different magnitudes it appears that the brightest are not always the nearest—(although, as might be expected, Alpha Centauri, the nearest, is one of the brightest in the heavens). Thus Sirius, the most brilliant of all the stars has not quite half the parallax of 61 Cygni, a star barely visible to the naked eye. We therefore conclude that Sirius is placed at a distance from the earth more than twice as great as that of 61 Cygni. Some of the brighter stars—for instance Alpha Cygni—show no perceptible parallax whatever!

ON THE DISTANCES OF THE FIXED STARS.

A parallax of one second of arc implies a distance from the earth equal to 206,265 times the earth's mean distance from the sun, or about 19 billions of miles, an extent of space which it is almost impossible for the mind to grasp, and which may be best expressed by stating that light, which takes about $8\frac{1}{4}$ minutes to travel from the sun to the earth, would not reach us from the nearest fixed star in less than $4\frac{1}{3}$ years! As, however, there are many stars—and some of them among the brightest in the heavens—which show no measurable parallax whatever, we can form no estimate of their actual distance from our system, and for anything we know to the contrary the light emitted by some of the fainter ones may take several hundred years to reach the earth. It has been even suggested by some writers that there may exist some stars at such a vast distance from the earth that their light may not have yet reached us, though travelling continually through space since their creation! This, however, seems highly improbable, and more probably light from such a distance would never reach us at all.

To gain some idea of the method employed in calculating the distance of a star from the earth let us consider the effect produced on the star's apparent place in the heavens caused by the earth's (annual) revolution round the sun. If an imaginary line be supposed drawn from the earth to the star, this line will describe in space a very elongated cone, having its vertex at the star, and its base the diameter of the earth's orbit round the sun. In consequence of this motion the star will apparently describe a small ellipse in the heavens; the diameter of this ellipse in angular measure being the vertical angle of the cone (see diagram, Fig. 1), or the angle subtended at the star by the diameter of the earth's orbit. *Half* this angle is the quantity to which the term parallax is applied, and it is evident that the smaller this angle is the greater the star's distance from the earth. For a star near the pole of the ecliptic it is clear that the small apparent ellipse described by the star will become a circle, or very nearly so. For a star near the ecliptic, or in the plane of the earth's orbit, this ellipse will become a straight line. For intermediate positions the greater axis of the ellipse will remain constant, but the minor axis will be shortened in the ratio of the sine of the latitude, or angular distance of the star from the ecliptic.

In the case of two stars apparently near each other, and situated at about the same distance from the earth, each would describe its own ellipse due to parallax, and their relative position would remain unaltered (unless, of course, they were in orbital motion) by the earth's change of position. If, however, one of the stars—though (seemingly) situated near to the other—is in reality placed at an immensely greater distance, the two stars will describe ellipses

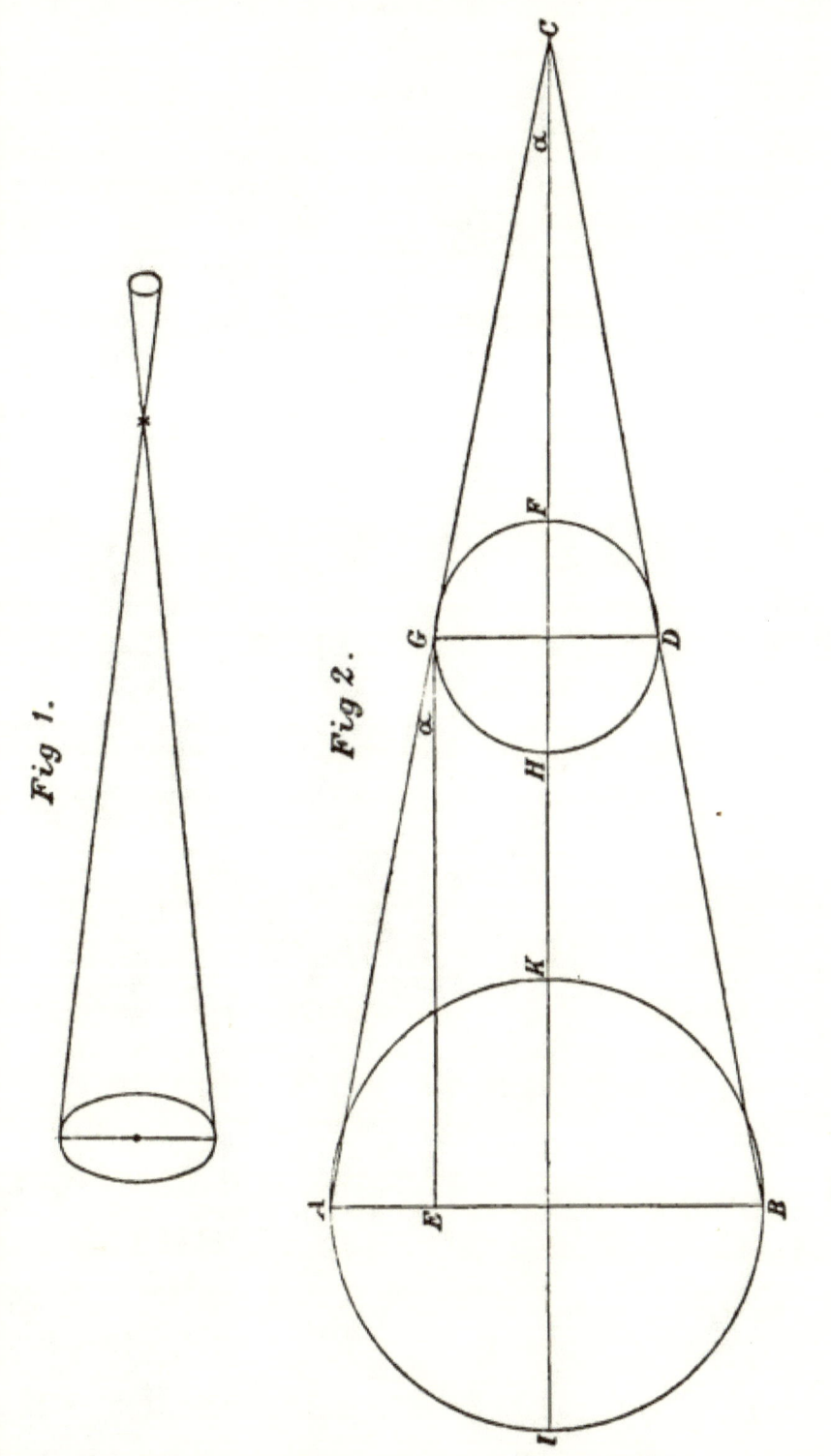

ON THE DISTANCES OF THE FIXED STARS.

differing in magnitude, owing to the differences in their parallaxes. If, then, the parallax of the nearer star be too small to measure directly, we may still arrive at an estimate of its amount by observing the relative positions of the two stars at different times of the year, as will be understood by the following diagram (in which however the relative motions are considerably exaggerated for the sake of clearness) in which the larger circle represents the ellipse described by the nearer star, and the smaller that by the more distant. Then as both stars will always be similarly situated in their parallactic ellipses, when one is at A the other will be at G; when one is at K, the other will be at F; when one is at B, other will be at D; and when one is at I, the other will be at H. The total variation, therefore, in the position of the line joining the two stars will be measured by the angle A C B. As this angle can be accurately measured with a micrometer, we can deduce the difference of parallax between the two stars, or the *relative* parallax, as it is called, of the nearer star (see Appendix, Note K).

It was by this method that the parallax of 61 Cygni was obtained by Bessel. Not far from this star are two very small stars which were chosen as suitable objects to compare with the brighter, and therefore probably the nearer star. Their relative positions were found to vary with such regularity that no doubt could be entertained that the observed motions were caused by a parallax in 61 Cygni, which—owing to the large amount of its proper motion—had been previously suspected of proximity to our system. The parallax found was little over one-third of a second, but recent researches have increased this to about 0·45 of a second. The distance of this star is therefore so vast that light, with its almost inconceivable velocity, will take more than 7 years to pass over the space which separates it from the earth! A few other small stars show parallaxes from $\frac{1}{4}$ to $\frac{1}{2}$ a second, or greater than that of Sirius, so that here we have the curious result that the brightest star in the heavens is actually farther from the earth than some stars invisible to the naked eye! This fact affords strong evidence in favour of Proctor's view that the brilliancy of a star is no test of its distance, and that probably some of the small stars composing the Milky Way may actually be nearer the earth than many of the brighter stars. From the large number of lucid stars visually projected on the Milky Way, he considers it probable that they are in reality intermixed with the smaller stars, and owe their greater brightness, not to relative proximity to the earth, but to real superiority in size.

THE MILKY WAY.

XV.

THE MILKY WAY.

In September, 1872, observing with the naked eye in the Punjab at a height of over 6,000 feet on the Himalayahs, I noticed a remarkable vacuity in the Milky Way in Cygnus not shown in Proctor's Atlas. If a line be supposed drawn from γ Cygni through α Cygni (Deneb) it will pass through this vacuity at about the same distance from α that α is from γ. The small double star Piazzi 429 is near the Southern boundary of this "coal sack," from which a dark rift passes across the Milky Way between the stars ξ and ρ Cygni. These remarks refer of course merely to naked-eye observation, as even with a small telescope I have seen numerous small stars scattered over the space referred to. In the clear air of the Himalayahs this dark spot is particularly noticeable, and immediately attracts the eye when directed to that portion of the sky. I subsequently found that the vacuity described above is shown in Heis'

Atlas, but he altogether omits the "dark rift," which seems quite as conspicuous.

In March, 1873, in the Punjab, I noticed a very faint offshoot from the Milky Way towards Orion. It apparently coincided very nearly with the stream of stars marked o^2, π^2, π^1, π^3, π^5, and π^6 in Proctor's Atlas (Map 4) between Aldebaran and Rigel. Heis does not show this extension of the Milky Way in his Atlas, but probably it is only to be seen on exceptionally clear nights in latitudes South of Europe.

THE GREAT PYRAMID

AND THE

PRECESSION

OF

THE EQUINOXES.

XVI.

THE GREAT PYRAMID AND THE PRECESSION OF THE EQUINOXES.[1]

I HAVE lately (1875) had the pleasure of meeting a gentleman whose favourite subject is the Great Pyramid, and who endeavoured to prove that this mighty monument of ancient architectural skill was built by Divine inspiration! I do not deny that the work was probably constructed for a special purpose, and that many of the curious numerical relations which have been discovered were doubtless intended by the builders, but in some of these relations there is much room for doubt, and in one or two cases on which the Pyramidalists lay particular stress it may be shown that the observed relations are purely accidental and could not possibly have been intended by the builders. In fact, as a well-known writer has said, the evidence seems "too strong for the occasion." But I do not so much take exception to the theories concerning the Pyramid held by the gentleman

[1] Published in *The Delhi Gazette*, March, 1875.

alluded to, as to a theory advanced by him to explain the well-known phenomenon known as the Precession of the Equinoxes, which is supposed, but erroneously, to be indicated by some of the Pyramid measures. This phenomenon which causes the pole of the equator to revolve round the pole of the ecliptic in a period of over 25,000 years, is due, as many of my readers are probably aware, to the attraction of the sun and moon on the protuberant matter at the earth's equator, which gives the polar axis of the earth a conical motion—like a teetotum when about to fall. This is the mathematical explanation of the phenomenon, and granting that the shape of the earth is—as is universally admitted—an oblate spheroid, it may be shown mathematically that such a motion *must* take place under the force of the solar and lunar attraction. Observation tells us that this motion *does* take place, so that here we have theory and observation in perfect accordance. The gentleman alluded to, however, would insist (and I suppose some other Pyramidalists believe in the same theory) that the phenomenon is caused by the revolution of the sun in an immense orbit round some central body in a period of about 25,000 years. As some readers may possibly have been misled by the arguments of Pyramidalists I give the following calculations, which will, I think, show the utterly untenable nature of this unnecessary hypothesis. Assuming (as he admits) the sun's annual velocity through space to be about 150 millions of miles (a velocity slightly greater or less will not affect my argument), and 25,000 years as the precessional period, we have 150,000,000 × 25,000 = 3,750,000,000,000 miles, which is (on this theory) the circumference of the orbit described by the sun round the central body. Now dividing this by 3·1416 (the ratio of the circumference to the diameter of a circle), we obtain 1,193,600,000,000 miles (roughly) as the diameter of the solar orbit, and one half of this, or 596,800,000,000 miles as the radius of the orbit, that is, the distance of the sun (or earth which comes to the same thing) from the hypothetical central body. This is of course on the supposition that the mass of the central body is so great with reference to the sun itself that it would practically remain immovable in the centre (as in the case of the sun and earth). Supposing however the sun and central body to be nearly equal in mass, both bodies would revolve round their common centre of gravity (which would of course be midway between them). The distance of the body found above would then require to be multiplied by 2, or in fact the diameter of the orbit first found would represent the distance of the hypothetical body from the earth. This, be it noted, is the maximum distance, assuming that the sun's annual motion is correctly determined. Greater than this it cannot be (if the laws of gravitation must be accepted). Now this distance is only about

$\frac{1}{20}$th of the distance of the nearest fixed star (*a* Centauri), a distance which has been fairly well determined and verified by different observers and computers, and which admits of no reasonable doubt. This star, *a* Centauri, is a large star of the 1st magnitude, and the combined mass of its components (it is a binary or revolving double star) is about $1\frac{3}{4}$ times the mass of the sun (another fact which no one competent to form an opinion on the matter would deny). Now placed at the same distance the sun would shine only as a star of about the 2nd magnitude, but placed at only $\frac{1}{20}$th of the distance, as above determined, it would—as light varies inversely as the square of the distance—probably vastly exceed Sirius in brilliancy. If such a body exists why is it not visible? To get over this difficulty the paradoxer would probably reply, "It may be a dark body." But we have nothing to warrant us in making any such assumption.

Again, as the whole circumference of 360° is described in 25,000 years, the apparent annual motion of the central body, or its "proper motion" as it is termed, would be about 50 seconds of arc. Now there is no star known in the heavens having so large a motion as this, the greatest proper motion yet detected being only about 7 seconds. Sirius, which from its great brilliancy might be looked upon with suspicion, has a proper motion of less than a second. Again, the annual parallax, or apparent change of place caused by the revolution of the earth round the sun, would necessarily amount to about 15 seconds of arc—an unheard-of quantity.

Besides the theory will not even account for the observed phenomenon. For, taking the parallax of the Pole star as 1 second (it is certainly very much less),[1] the change of place caused by the sun's motion in its orbit would only amount to about $3\frac{1}{2}$ degrees on each side of the pole, whereas observation shows the actual amount to be about $23\frac{1}{2}$ degrees. These considerations justify us, I think, in rejecting the theory as resting on an unproved assumption, and altogether inferior to the physical theory which ascribes the phenomenon to the attraction of the sun and moon on the excess of matter at the earth's equator, a theory which has the support of all the ablest living mathematicians, some of them not inferior to Newton in intellect.

[1] Prof. Pritchard finds by photography $0''\cdot 052 \pm 0''\cdot 0314$.

CHANGES IN THE STELLAR HEAVENS.

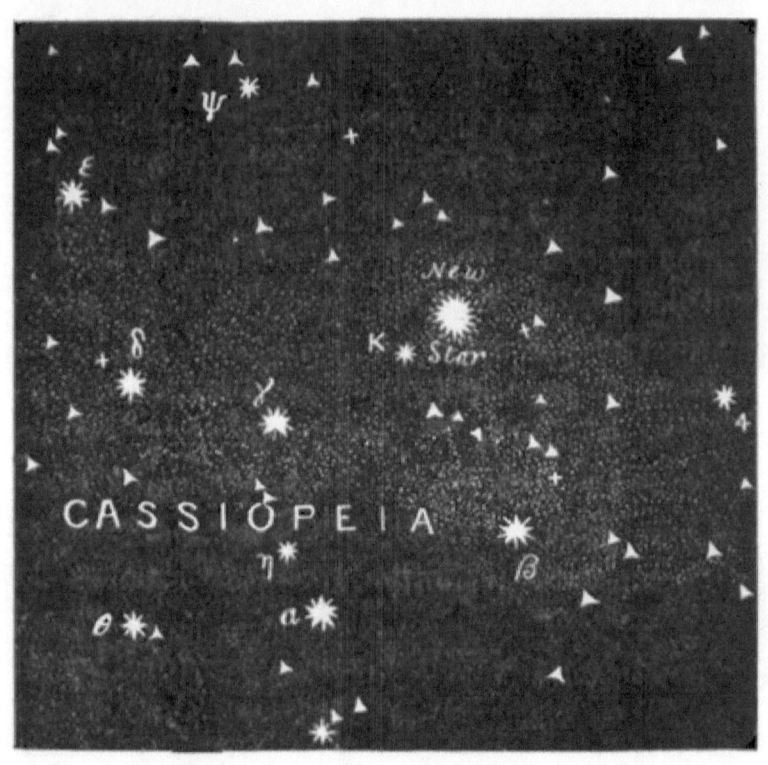

THE TEMPORARY STAR OF 1572.

XVII.

CHANGES IN THE STELLAR HEAVENS.

If we look up at the starry heavens on a clear moonless night all seems still, lifeless, and devoid of energy and motion. All of us are, or at least should be, familiar with the apparent diurnal motion of the star sphere, caused by the *real* rotation of the earth on its axis, and with the slower annual motion, due to the earth's revolution round the sun, which brings different constellations into view at different seasons of the year. These motions, due to the great and universal law of gravitation, discovered and so ably expounded by the famous Sir Isaac Newton, are of course wonderful and orderly in their regularity, and bear silent testimony to the amazing power, majesty, and goodness of a great and glorious Creator. There are, however, other motions and changes, even still more wonderful, going on in the depths of space which though unperceived by the ordinary observer have been revealed to the eye and contemplation of the astronomer by the accurate instruments and methods of research which modern science has placed at his disposal. Some account of these marvellous discoveries may prove of interest to the general reader. The "fixed stars" are so called, because they apparently hold a fixed position with reference to each other on the concave surface of the celestial vault, and do not, as far as the unaided eye can judge, change their relative positions as the planets do. Many stars have, however, what is technically called a "proper motion," which, though of course very minute, and only to be detected by the aid of refined and accurate instruments, yet accumulate in the course of ages, and appreciably alter their position in the sky. The largest "proper motion" hitherto detected (about seven seconds of arc per annum) is that of a small star in the constellation Ursa Major, known to astronomers as No. 1830 of Groombridge's Catalogue. It has been calculated that this star is rushing through space with the amazing and almost inconceivable velocity of 200 miles per second! a velocity which would carry it from the earth to the sun in about $5\frac{1}{2}$ days and to the moon in 20 minutes! The well-known double star 61 Cygni has a proper motion of about five seconds of arc per annum, both components moving through space together. This is as far as yet known, the nearest star to the earth in the northern hemisphere. Its parallax, as determined by Sir R. S. Ball is 0·4676 of a second of arc, and by Professor

Pritchard (by photography) 0·43 of a second. Taking the mean of these values, its distance from the earth would be about 460,000 times the earth's mean distance from the sun, and its actual velocity about 33 miles per second. This is of course the motion at right angles to the line of sight, but as it may also have a motion *in* the line of sight—either to or from the eye—its real velocity is probably greater than this. The remarkable triple star 40 Eridani has a proper motion of four seconds annually. The components are a 4th magnitude star accompanied by a distant double companion, which is a binary or revolving double star (of which the orbit has been computed by the present writer), and accompanies the bright star in its flight through space. There are two other faint and distant companions which do not partake in the motion of the ternary star. In the year 1864 the bright star was situated to the east of a line joining these faint companions, but owing to the large proper motion it is now to the west of them—an interesting phenomenon.[1] In the case of the triple star Struve 1516, one of the companions which was to the west of the primary star in 1831 is, owing to the proper motion of the bright star, now to the east of it. Professor Asaph Hall has found a parallax for 40 Eridani of 0·223 of a second. This, combined with the observed proper motion, indicates an actual velocity of about 54 miles per

[1] "Journal Liverpool Astronomical Society," vol v. p. 140.

second. The proper motion of the bright star Arcturus is so considerable that in the course of about 32,000 years it will be near the equator, and a little to the east of Zeta Virginis, and close to a small star which is now to the west of Zeta. It will then usurp the place of Spica as the brighest star in Virgo. In about 16,000 years hence Sirius will be very close to the 4th magnitude star known as ξ^1 in Canis Major which is at present about 7 degrees to the south of it. After about the same lapse of time Procyon, the bright star in the Little Dog, will be a little to the east of the star 22 Monocerotis. The triple star Mu Cassiopeiæ in 44,000 years hence will form one of the Pleiades! This star about 4,000 years ago must have been close to Alpha Cassiopeiæ, and might have been so seen by the ancient astronomers. These motions are of course those which take place across the face of the sky. There are, however, motions in the line of sight both towards and from the eye—which have of late years been revealed to us by the spectroscope, that wonderful instrument of modern scientific research, by the aid of which several new metals have been discovered, and which has been found so useful in chemical analysis and even in the manufacture of steel by the Bessemer process. Some years since Dr. Huggins the eminent spectroscopist found that Sirius "the monarch of the skies" was receding from the earth at the rate of about 20 miles a second. Later observations at Greenwich observatory showed that this motion was gradually diminishing, and within the last few years it has been found that the motion of recession has been actually changed into a motion of approach, showing that this giant sun is probably travelling in a mighty orbit round some, as yet unknown, centre of gravity.

From a consideration of stellar proper motions it has been concluded that the sun—and therefore the whole Solar System—is moving through space with a considerable velocity. The earlier determinations place the point towards which the sun is moving in the constellation Hercules. Recent researches make the velocity of translation about 19 miles per second (30 kilometres). The Greenwich observations place the "apex of the solar motion" between Rho and Sigma Cygni, while Dr. Huggins' results fix a point near Beta Cephei. Both these points are near the Milky Way.[1] Later researches, however, by L. Struve place the apex in the constellation Hercules, not far from the point fixed by the earlier calculations.[2]

There are other startling changes which have occasionally taken place among the stars, and which must be looked upon almost in the light of catastrophes. At rare intervals in the history of astronomy "temporary" or "new stars" have suddenly blazed out in the heavens, which were pre-

[1] *Naturalists' Monthly*, January, 1888.
[2] See Appendix, Note M.

viously either unknown stars to astronomers, or else were invisible, except in the telescope. Some of those recorded in the annals of astronomy were of great brilliancy, that observed by Tycho Brahé in 1572 having been visible in broad daylight. The first of these extraordinary objects of which we have any account is one recorded in the Chinese annals as having appeared in the year B.C. 134 in the constellation Scorpio. The historian Pliny tells us that it was the sudden appearance of a new star which led the astronomer Hipparchus to form his catalogue of stars, the first ever constructed. As the date of Hipparchus' catalogue is B.C. 125, it seems probable that the star referred to was identical with that mentioned in the Chinese annals as having been seen nine years previously.

The next object is one which is said to have appeared between a and δ in Ursa Major in the year B.C. 76, but no details of its appearance seem to have been recorded.

In the year 101 A.D. a small "yellowish blue" star is said to have appeared in the well-known "sickle" in Leo, but the description leaves its exact position very doubtful.

In A.D. 107 a strange star is recorded near δ, ϵ, and η Canis Majoris. These three stars form a triangle south-east of Sirius.

In A.D. 123 a star is recorded to have blazed out near a Herculis and a Ophinchi.

On December 10, 173, a bright star is recorded in the Chinese annals as having appeared between α and β Centauri (two bright stars in the southern hemisphere). It remained visible for seven or eight months, and is described as resembling "a large bamboo mat" (!)—a not very lucid description. It is worthy of remark that there exists at the present time, close to the spot, a remarkable red and variable star—R Centauri—which varies from the 6th to the 10th magnitude, and which may possibly be identical with the star of the Chinese annals.

"Strange stars" are mentioned in the years 290, 304, and 369 A.D., but the accounts given are very vague and their position very uncertain. In the year 386 A.D. a new star was seen near λ, μ and ψ Sagittarii. As the place indicated is near the position of a missing star, which was observed by Flamsteed, and called by him 65 Ophiuchi, it has been thought possible that Flamsteed's star may have been a return of the star recorded in the Chinese annals.

Cuspianus relates that in the year 389 A.D. a star as bright as Venus appeared near α Aquilæ (Altair). It remained visible only three weeks. Lynn considers, however, that this was probably a comet.

In the year 393 A.D. a strange star is recorded near μ^2 Scorpii. In 561 A.D. an extraordinary star was seen near α Crateris. A known variable and red star —R Crateris—lies close to this position.

In 829 A.D. the Chinese annals note a star somewhere near the bright star Procyon (α Canis Minoris). There are several variable stars in this vicinity, one of which may possibly be identical with the star in question.

Leoviticus, in his work, "De Conjunctionibus Magnus," mentions a new star near Cassiopeia in the year 945 A.D. It has been surmised that this star was an apparition of Tycho Brahé's star of 1572; a star also mentioned by Leoviticus as having appeared in 1264 being considered another appearance of the same object. But it has been shown by Lynn and Sadler that the supposed stars of 945 and 1264 were most probably comets.

An extraordinary star is recorded as having appeared near ζ Sagittarii in the year 1011 A.D., and another in 1203, near μ^2 Scorpii. Another is recorded near π Scorpii on July 1, 1584. The number of these objects recorded in this portion of the sky is remarkable.

Hepidannus mentions a star in Aries in 1012, as being of an astonishing size, and "dazzling the eye" (!).

Temporary stars are recorded as having been seen in 1054 A.D., south-east of ζ Tauri, and in 1139 near κ Virginis, but the accounts are very vague.

We now come to the very remarkable star observed in Cassiopeia by the famous astronomer, Tycho Brahé. He has left on record a very elaborate account of his observations of this wonderful object, his description covering no less than 478 pages of printed matter, one of the most remarkable astronomical monographs ever published. The discovery of the star was made on November 9th by Cornelius Gemma, who states that it was not visible on November 8th in a clear sky. The attention of Tycho Brahé was, however, first attracted to the star on November 11th. It increased rapidly in brilliancy until it surpassed Jupiter and rivalled Venus in brightness, when it was visible in the daytime. This state of things was not, however, of long duration, as it gradually diminished in lustre, and in March, 1574, had completely disappeared, at least to the naked eye. Its curious changes are thus described: "As it decreased in size so it varied in colour; at first its light was white and extremely bright; it then became yellowish, afterwards of a ruddy colour, and finished with a pale livid colour."

According to the position deduced by Argelander from Tycho Brahé's observations, and which is confirmed by a sketch given in Tycho Brahé's work (referred to above), the star, which was called "The Pilgrim," was situated about $1\frac{1}{2}$ degrees north of Kappa Cassiopeia, which is the faintest star in the well-known "Chair." This spot is very devoid of stars to the naked eye, and even in a binocular only a few faint stars are visible. Within one minute of arc (a space quite imperceptible to the naked eye) of the place fixed by Argelander, d'Arrest in 1865 observed a small star of the 11th magnitude, which seems not to have been seen by Argelander. According to observations by Hind and Plummer in 1873, this small star shows signs of unsteadiness in its light to the extent of nearly one magnitude. The star has also been observed by Espin. It may be readily identified by means of a bright 9th magnitude which is No. 22 of Argelander's zone 60; it follows this 9th magnitude by 29·6 seconds, and is south of 10' 4"·1. It should be carefully watched, as it may possibly prove to be identical with the long-lost star of Tycho Brahé. According to Schönfeld, the hypothesis of its identity with the Star of Bethlehem has been supported by Cardanus, Chladni, and Klinkerfues, but this theory has been shown by Lynn and Sadler to be quite untenable, and has now been abandoned by astronomers.

The next object worthy of notice is the very remarkable one observed by Kepler in October, 1604, in Ophiuchus, and described by him in his work, "De Stella Nova in pede Serpentarii." The planets, Mars, Jupiter, and Saturn, were near each other in this region of the heavens (a few degrees south-east of the star Eta Ophiuchi); and one evening Möstlin, a pupil of Kepler's, remarked that a new and very brilliant star had joined the group. When first seen it was white, and exceeded in brilliancy Mars and Jupiter, and was even thought to rival Venus in splendour! It gradually diminished, and in six months was not equal in lustre to Saturn. In March, 1606, it had entirely disappeared. It was also observed by Galileo. The position assigned to this star by Schönfeld, from the observations of David Fabricius, places it about midway between the 5th magnitude stars ξ and 58 Ophiuchi. There does not, however, seem to be the same amount of certainty with reference to its exact position, as in the case of Tycho Brahé's star in Cassiopeia, nor is there any star within two minutes of arc of the place determined by Schönfeld, the nearest being one of the 12th magnitude, a little *south following*. Chacornac, however, in 1861, mapped a star of the 10th magnitude about 2 minutes preceding the spot, and this star was missed by some observers in 1871 and 1872. Professor Winnecke in 1875 observed a star of the 12th magnitude very near the place of Chacornac's star. Sadler has, however, since pointed out that Chacornac's star is identical with a star of the 9th magnitude which follows by about 6 minutes of arc the place of the Nova, the star having been misplaced on Chacornac's maps owing to distortion in the scale near the edges of the charts. It seems possible that Kepler's star may have been seen by Ptolemy, as Baily, in his edition of Ptolemy's catalogue says, with reference to Ptolemy's No. 13 in Ophiuchus "longitude 26° 20' or 23° 40'. If the latter, the star is 40 Ophiuchi, but all the other copies have 26° 40', which would place the star in the position of the *stella nova* discovered by Kepler. The magnitude given by Ptolemy is δ or 4th magnitude."

With reference to this star it may be worthy of notice that on the morning of December 21, 1882, several persons at Broughty Ferry noticed a bright star in close proximity to the sun. At the time of the observation the place of Kepler's star was only about eight degrees from the sun's place, so that if the object seen was really a star (and not a comet) it seems not improbable that it may have been a return of Kepler's star (see *Knowledge*, December 29, 1882, and January 5, 1883).

In the year 1612 a new star is said to have appeared in Aquila. Klein thinks this is identical with one mentioned by the Chinese in 1609.

In 1670 a star of the third magnitude was observed by Anthelm near β Cygni. It remained visible for about two years, and increased and diminished several times before it finally disappeared. Its exact position has been computed by Schönfeld from the observations of Hevelius and Picard. Within one minute of arc of this place a star of the 11th magnitude has been meridianally observed at Greenwich Observatory. Hind and others suspect variability in this small star. In August, 1872, it was exactly equal to a star which follows it; while in November, 1874, it was certainly fainter by half a magnitude.[1] According to Hind the suspicious

[1] *Nature*, June, 1877.

star precedes Lalande's star No. 37730 by 25 seconds of time in Right Ascension, and is about 23 minutes of arc to the south of it. He says that to his eye "there is a hazy, ill-defined appearance about it which is not perceptible in other stars in the same field of view. Mr. Talmage received the same impression; and I may add that Mr. Baxendell, who has examined it with Mr. Worthington's reflector, observed that no adjustment of focus would bring the star up to a sharp focus." This seems suggestive, as the star may possibly be a small planetary nebula similar to Schmidt's Nova in Cygnus (1876). Hind also remarks that the known variable star S Vulpeculæ, which follows the star alluded to, has been shown to have no proper motion to account for the difference of position since 1670. " From the fixity of its position during eight years it may be inferred that the variable is distinct from Anthelm's."

The star 11 Vulpeculæ of Flamsteed has been supposed to be identical with Anthelm's star. Baily could not find that Flamsteed's star ever really existed, but says: "Under the presumption, however, that it may be a variable and not a *lost* star, I have preserved its recorded position with a view of inducing astronomers to look out for it from time to time."

A small temporary star was observed by Hind in Ophiuchus on April 28, 1848. When first noticed it was about 5th magnitude. It afterwards rose to nearly 4th magnitude, but very soon faded to 10th or 11th magnitude. Hind is convinced that up to April 3rd or 5th, no object of $9\frac{1}{2}$ magnitude or brighter was visible in its position. There are several small stars near the place of the Nova. This curious object has become very faint in recent years. In 1866 it was 12th magnitude; and in 1874 and 1875 not above 13th magnitude. Its position is marked in Proctor's Atlas, Map 9.

A new star was discovered by Pogson, May 28, 1860, in the globular cluster known as 80 Messier in Scorpio. When first seen it was about 7th magnitude, and bright enough to obscure the nebula in which it was apparently situated. On June 10th the star had nearly disappeared, and the nebula again shone with great brilliancy and with a condensed centre. Pogson's observations were confirmed by Auwers and Luther. It was stated by Pogson that he examined the nebula on May 9th, and found nothing remarkable; and, according to Schönfeld, on May 18th it presented its usual appearance in the Heliometer of the Königsberg Observatory. Some trace of the object seems to have been since seen by Schönfeld, June 1, 1869.

A very interesting "temporary" star—now known as the "Blaze Star" suddenly appeared in Corona Borealis in May, 1866. It was first seen by Birmingham at Tuam, Ireland, about midnight on the evening of May 12th, when it was of the 2nd magnitude, and equal to Alphecca, the brightest star in the well-known "Coronet." It was shortly after noticed by several observers in different parts of the world. The appearance must have taken place very suddenly as Schmidt, the Director of the Athens Observatory, stated that he was observing the region on the same evening about $2\frac{1}{2}$ hours previous to Birmingham's discovery, and that no star of even the 5th magnitude could possibly have escaped his notice. The star rapidly diminished in brightness, and on May 24th of the same year had faded to $8\frac{1}{2}$ magnitude. It afterwards increased to nearly 7th magnitude, but soon diminished again. It was soon discovered that the star was not really a new one, but had been observed previously by Schönfeld at Bonn in 1855 and 1856, and registered as $9\frac{1}{2}$ magnitude on both occasions. When near its maximum brilliancy its light was examined by Dr. Huggins with the spectroscope, which showed the bright lines of hydrogen gas in addition to the ordinary stellar spectrum. This implies that the great increase in its light was chiefly due to a sudden outburst of hydrogen gas in the star's atmosphere. Some observers remarked that when viewed with the naked eye it decidedly twinkled more than other stars near it, which rendered a correct estimation of its relative brightness very difficult. During the period 1866 to 1876 Schmidt detected variations of light which seemed to exhibit a certain regularity. He deduces from his observations a probable period of about 94 days. This conclusion has been confirmed by Schönfeld who has observed changes in the star from about the 7th to the 9th magnitude. The star appears therefore to be an irregular variable. It is situated a little south of Epsilon Coronæ Borealis, and its position is marked in Proctor's Atlas, Map 8.

A still more extraordinary object was discovered by Schmidt at Athens near Rho Cygni,[1] on the evening of November 24, 1876, when it was about the 3rd magnitude, and somewhat brighter than Eta Pegasi. It did not however remain long at this brightness, but rapidly diminished, and on November 30th had descended to the 5th magnitude. It was remarked that on the night of its discovery its brightness was such as to render its near neighbour 75 Cygni invisible, while on December 14th and 15th, 75 Cygni (a 6th magnitude star) in its turn nearly obliterated the light of the stranger. In the 48 hours following the night of November 27th and 28th the star diminished in light to the extent of nearly 1½ magnitude (!) It afterwards diminished very regularly to August, 1877, exhibiting no oscillations of brightness, as have been observed in other new stars. On the evening of its discovery Schmidt considered the star to be of a strong golden yellow, and that it afterwards remained a deep yellow, but at no time was it as ruddy as the

[1] See Sketch.

neighbouring 75 Cygni. Schmidt observed the vicinity on several occasions between November 1st and November 20th, and is certain that no star of even 5th magnitude could have escaped his notice, so that the new star must have blazed out very suddenly. Between November 20th and 24th the sky was cloudy,

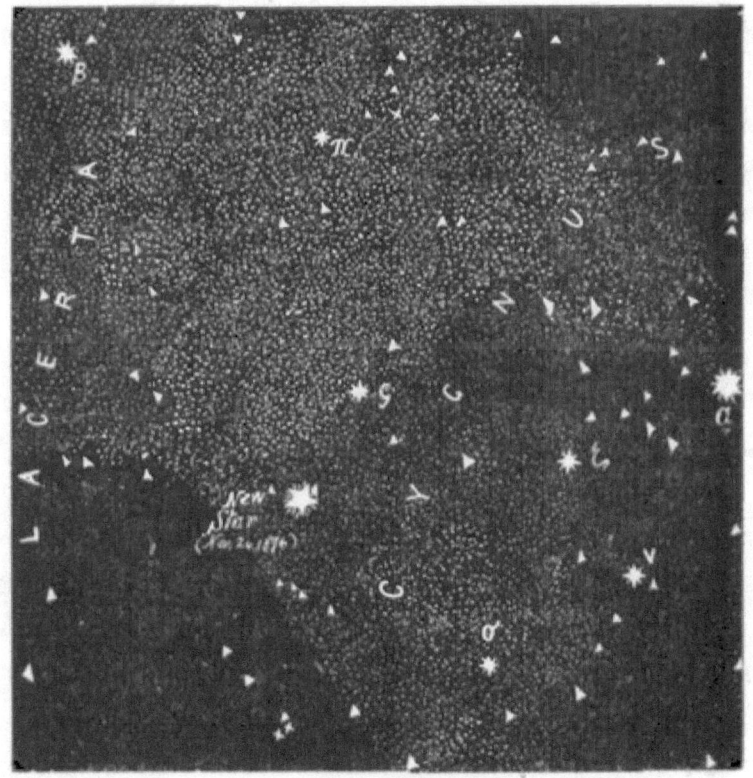

NEW STAR IN CYGNUS.

so the exact time of its appearance is unknown. It was spectroscopically examined a few days after its discovery and showed bright lines similar to the star in Corona Borealis. One of the bright lines was believed to be identical with the line numbered 1474 by Kirchoff, visible in the spectrum of the solar corona during total eclipses of the sun. The other bright lines were identified by M. Cornu, of the Paris Observatory, with some of the lines of hydrogen, sodium, and magnesium of the solar spectrum. The star would seem to be quite new, as there is no star in any of the catalogues in the position of the Nova, the nearest being one of the 9th magnitude which is found in the Bonn observations. When the star had faded to the 7th magnitude it was thought by some observers to be colourless, whereas by others it was considered decidedly orange. I could see no trace of colour in the star with a 3-inch refractor on January 12, 1877 (when first seen by me in the Punjab), but it had then faded to the 8th magnitude. On February 7, 1877, I estimated it 9th magnitude. In September, 1877, the star was examined with a 15-inch refractor by Lord Lindsay (now Lord Crawford), who found "the light coming from it almost entirely monochromatic (of only one colour) the star appearing exactly the same as when looked at without the spectroscope, the direct prism having no effect on it. He considers that there is little doubt but that this star has changed into a planetary nebula of small angular diameter" (!) On September 3rd the magnitude was $10\frac{1}{2}$; "faint blue near another star of same size, rather red." Lord Crawford remarks that no observer discovering the object in its present state would, after viewing it through a prism, hesitate to pronounce as to its nebulous character, but no disc has been detected with powers ranging up to 1000 or 1100 diameters. Vogel, however, considers that the theory of the star having changed into a planetary nebula is inadmissible, as the most characteristic of the three nebular lines (the second) was not seen at all when the spectrum was very bright. Backhouse, however, observed a line in the spectrum at about wave length 4960, which agrees fairly well in position with the second nebular line. This, however, rapidly faded out, and the spectrum was ultimately reduced to a line whose wave length was 5022. Ward found the star only 16th magnitude in October, 1881, and it was estimated 15th magnitude with the $15\frac{1}{2}$-inch refractor of Mr. Wigglesworth's observatory in September, 1885. At Lord Crawford's observatory the position of the Nova with reference to above 50 closely adjacent stars has been carefully determined with the micrometer.

In August, 1885, a star of about 7th magnitude made its appearance close to the nucleus of the Great Nebula in Andromeda (Messier 31), a well-known object visible to the naked eye, and which has been well called "the Queen of the Nebulæ." The new star was independently discovered by several observers towards the end of August. It was not visible to Temple at the Florence Observatory on August 15th and 16th, and is said to have been seen on August 17th by M. Ludovic Gully. It was, however, certainly seen by Mr. I. W. Ward, of Belfast, on August 19th at 11 p.m., when he estimated it $9\frac{1}{2}$ magnitude, and it was independently detected by M. Lajoye on August 30th; by Dr. Hartwig at Dorpat on August 31st, and by Mr. G. T. Davis at Theale, near Reading, on September 1st. On September 3rd the star was observed as $7\frac{1}{2}$ magnitude at Dun Echt by Lord Crawford, and Dr. Copeland, and its spectrum was found to be "fairly continuous." On September 4th, Mr. Maunder at the Greenwich Observatory, found the spectrum "of precisely the same character as that of the nebula, *i.e.*, it was perfectly continuous, no lines, either bright or dark being visible, and the red end was wanting." Dr. Huggins, however, on September 9th, thought he could see from three to five bright lines in its spectrum. The star gradually faded away, and on February 7, 1886, was estimated only 16th magnitude with the 26-inch refractor of the Naval Observatory at Washington. From a series of measures by Professor Asaph Hall he found "no certain indications of any parallax," so that evidently the star and the nebula in which it probably lies are situated at an immense distance from the earth. Professor Seeliger has investigated the decrease in the light of this star on the hypothesis that it was a cooling body which had been suddenly raised to an intense heat by the shock of a collision, and finds a fair agreement between theory and observation. Auwers points out the similarity between this outburst and the new star of 1860 in the cluster 80 Messier, and thinks it very probable that both phenomenon were due to physical changes in the nebulæ in which they occurred.

A reddish star of the sixth magnitude was discovered by the present writer near χ' Orionis on the evening of Dec. 13, 1885. This star, previously unknown to astronomers, was at first thought to be a " temporary star," and called *Nova Orionis*, but subsequent observations have shown that it is an ordinary long period variable, of the type of Mira Ceti, with a period of about a year. At minimum it descends to about $12\frac{1}{2}$ magnitude. Its spectrum is a splendid specimen of Secchi's third type.[1]

The cause of these wonderful phenomena is doubtful, but from the spectroscopic observation of the temporary stars of 1866 and 1876, it seems probable that — in some cases at least — the extraordinary increase in their light is due to an outburst of hydrogen and other combustible gases in the atmosphere of the star, possibly produced by the heat caused by collision with some dark body or flight of meteors.

It seems not improbable that more of these wonderful objects may have appeared but escaped detection, owing to cloudy skies, &c. Most of them

[1] See next chapter.

remain but a few days at their maximum brilliancy—those of 1572 and 1604 being, however, notable exceptions.

A familiar acquaintance with the naked eye stars down to the fifth magnitude would soon show to an observer the presence of a stranger, almost at a glance; and were a number of observers to keep watch on one or two constellations each, comparing the stars with a good map (such as Heis') on every clear night, the number of temporary stars might possibly be considerably increased in a few years.[1]

It is worthy of remark that the great majority of these interesting objects have made their appearance in or near the Milky Way, the most remarkable exception to this rule being the star of 1866 in Corona Borealis.

With reference to the colours of the stars, some of the red stars have been suspected to vary in colour. The bright star Sirius is supposed—from the description of it by the ancient astronomers — to have been originally red, but this seems very doubtful. The Persian astronomer, Al-Sufi in his "Description of the Heavens," written in the tenth century, describes the well-known variable star, Algol, distinctly as a red star. It is now white, and this is perhaps the best attested instance on record of change of colour in a bright star.

[1] Proceedings, Liverpool Astronomical Society, Session 1882–83.

THE NEW STAR IN ORION.

XVIII.

THE NEW STAR IN ORION.

ON the evening of Dec. 13, 1885, at about 9 hours 20 minutes p.m., while examining the small stars in the northern portion of Orion with a binocular field-glass, my attention was arrested by the appearance of a reddish star of the 6th magnitude closely following the 5th magnitude star 54 (Flamsteed) Orionis. As there is no star in this position given by Lalande, Harding, Heis, or in Birmingham's Catalogue of red stars, I immediately suspected that it was a "new star." Next day I reported my observation to Dr. Copeland at Lord Crawford's Observatory, Dun Echt, Aberdeen, who fully confirmed the discovery. The star was observed at Dun Echt on the evening of Dec. 16th, and Dr. Copeland estimated it $6\frac{1}{2}$ magnitude, and of an orange red colour. Examined with the spectroscope he found "a very beautiful banded spectrum of the third type, seven dark bands being readily distinguished with the prism. The bright intervals seemed full of bright lines, especially in the green and blue." The star is not in Argelander's *Durchmusterung*, the nearest star being one of about the 9th magnitude, which lies about $3\frac{1}{2}$ minutes of arc south of the new star. Espin found a small companion about $10\frac{1}{2}$ magnitude, about 30 seconds of arc following. M. Wolf found that the supposed existence of bright lines was not confirmed when a spectroscope with higher dispersive power was used. He considers that the spectrum was simply that of the well-known third type, viz., a continuous spectrum crossed by bands bounded by dark and sharp edges towards the violet, and shading away towards the red. He partially resolved the dark bands into lines. Dr. Copeland identified three lines in the spectrum with the edges of three bands visible in the spectra of comets, and the spectrum of coal gas, but these views were disputed by Mr. Maunder. MM. Perrotin and Thollon, however, found a spectrum suggesting "a certain analogy with the spectra of comets, only more complicated." They concluded, however, that the spectrum was of the same type as that of a Orionis (Betelgeuse). Professor Riccò, at the Palermo Observatory, found a spectrum "very brilliant from the red to the blue, with six or eight brilliant bands decreasing in light to the violet, or the more refrangible side," and the maximum of light "always in the green."

Shortly after the discovery of the new star the

Rev. S. J. Johnson called attention to the fact that a star was shown in Bode's Maps (1782) near the position of the *Nova*. On examining the original records Dr. Copeland found that Bode refers the star to Hevel, and that it is No. 1064 of Baily's edition of Hevel's Catalogue. Baily, however, could not "find any star that will accord" with Hevel's position, and Dr. Copeland concludes that if Hevel really did observe the *Nova* there must be an error of 1° in Hevel's observation. This seems to show that probably Hevel's observations refer to some other object. Flamsteed observed the vicinity on Feb. 20, 1680, but makes no mention of any star near the place of the new one. It is not found in Al-Sufi or any of the ancient catalogues. The new star slowly diminished in light, and on March 3, 1886, was reduced to the 9th magnitude. It afterwards diminished to below the 12th magnitude in July, 1886, and it was then suspected that it was probably a variable star with a period of about one year. This proved to be the case, for it again increased in brightness during the autumn of 1886, and reached another maximum about Dec. 10th, of that year, but was then about half a magnitude fainter than on the night of its discovery. It then slowly faded again, and was about 9th magnitude in the middle of March, 1887. Another maximum was reached in December, 1887, but on this occasion it did not attain the 7th magnitude. It seems probable that it is a variable of the type of Mira Ceti, which at some maxima is much brighter than at others.

Lockyer considers that stars of the type of "Nova" Orionis and Alpha Orionis "are not masses of vapour like our sun, but clouds of incandescent stones, . . . probably the first stage of meteoritic condensation."

THE VARIABLE STAR μ CEPHEI.

XIX.

THE VARIABLE STAR μ CEPHEI.

This interesting variable—the "garnet star" of Sir William Herschel—was found to be variable by Hind in 1848, and the variability was confirmed by Argelander, who made numerous observations of it in the year 1848 to 1864. According to Schönfeld (*Zweiter Catalog von veränderlichen Sternen*, 1875) Argelander's observations give the formula—

Epoch E. Min. 1855, Oct. 15·6, Max. 1856, June 20·1 + 431·786d. E.

I have made over 160 observations of this star in the years 1883 to 1887, and find it certainly variable to the extent of a little over one magnitude, but with no regular period. Argelander's period of 431 days is not confirmed by my observations, which I think show that the variation cannot be represented by any fixed or mean period. Its red colour, and at times strong scintillation, render a correct estimate of its magnitude somewhat difficult. The observations were chiefly made with a binocular field-glass, having object glasses of two-inches aperture, and power of about six diameters. Occasionally when near a maximum, the star was also observed with the naked eye. Argelander's method of observation was used. The highest recorded magnitude was 3·6 on May 11, 1885, and the lowest 4·8 on Sept. 4, 1883. The star is therefore variable from 3·6 mag. to 4·8 mag.—in the scale of the Harvard Photometry. The variation is very irregular, the star sometimes remaining for several months at a time with scarcely any perceptible variation. The spectrum is a fine example of Secchi's third type. μ Cephei is No. 7582 of the British Association Catalogue of stars, and its position for 1890 is

R.A. 21h. 40m. 8s., N., 58° 16'·5d.

THE PROBABLE VARIABILITY
OF
BETA LEONIS.

XX.

ON THE PROBABLE VARIABILITY OF BETA LEONIS.

FROM the magnitudes assigned to this star, known as Denebola by the earlier astronomers, it seems probable that it has diminished in brightness. It was rated of the 1st magnitudes by Al-Sufi, Ptolemy, and Tycho Brahé, but only 2nd magnitude by Lalande, Argelander, Heis, and others. In the "Philosophical Transactions" for 1796 Sir W. Herschel rated it slightly less than Gamma Leonis, and remarks: "From the expressions of this catalogue, it is evident that the star is less now than it was 13 years ago. The magnitude of this star given by Flamsteed is 1-2, but as there is some ground to admit that this mag., even in this coarse way of reference, may be distinguished from what the same author seems to have taken for 2 mag., we conclude that this star has probably lost some of its former brightness. Again, he gives Beta 1·2 mag., and Gamma 2 mag. This notation seems to imply that Beta is larger than Gamma, which, not being the case, we have additional reason to suspect a change. De la Caille puts down Beta as 2 mag., though the difference between the notation of Flamsteed and the latter author can add little force to the argument for a change, as we have observed before, that a considerable allowance must be made for nominal variations in different authors. Nor can we draw any support from the magnitude itself, because the star will pass very well for one of that order when compared with other stars which are marked 2 mag. by the same author; but when De la Caille marks Beta 2 mag. and Gamma 3 mag., we may then conclude that he estimated Beta to be larger than Gamma though we do not know that he compared these two stars together, because a whole magnitude in the second class cannot well be mistaken, coarse as is the type to which the reference is made." If we consider that Beta and Gamma Leonis are not far distant in the sky, and that both stars were probably observed—at least by the earlier observers—at the same time, Sir W. Herschel's reasoning in favour of a diminution of light in Beta seems strengthened. The Persian astronomer Al-Sufi, writing in the middle of the tenth century speaks of it as "la première grandeur est la brillante et grande qui se trouve sur la queue" (Schjellerup's translation of the Persian MSS.), exactly similar words to those he uses in describing *a* Leonis (Regulus), so that probably

PROBABLE VARIABILITY OF BETA LEONIS.

it was then comparable in brightness to this well-known 1st magnitude star. Beta Leonis was measured with the "wedge photometer" at Oxford 2·07 mag., and with the meridian photometer at Harvard (U.S.A.) 2·23 mag., Regulus being 1·17 at Oxford, and 1·42 mag. at Harvard. Upon the the whole therefore, we may conclude that Beta Leonis is now less brilliant than it was formerly, and the star should be watched for fluctuations of light, as it may possibly be a variable star with a very long period. In February, 1885, and March, 1887, I found Beta perceptibly brighter than Gamma, although Beta was at lower altitude on both occasions.

A distant companion of the 8th magnitude, "dull red," was observed by Admiral Smyth in 1833. This small star seems to have since faded, as it was found only 11 mag. by Knott in 1878. In 1878 I observed with a 3-inch refractor, a small star about 11 mag., nearly in the position given by Smyth. Smyth mentions a distant 7 magnitude star *north preceding* Beta, but I saw a brighter and closer companion than this, of which Smyth makes no mention.

THE MASSES AND DISTANCES
OF THE
BINARY STARS.

XXI.

ON THE MASSES AND DISTANCES OF THE BINARY STARS.

When the parallax of a binary star is known (or its distance from the earth) and the elements of its orbit have been computed satisfactorily, it is easy to find the sum of the masses of the component stars in terms of the sun's mass and the real dimensions of the orbit. For if P be the period of revolution of the binary in years, d the semi-axis major of the orbit (or the mean distance) in terms of the sun's mean distance from the earth, m and m^1 the masses of the components, and M the sun's mass, we have from the laws of orbital motion.

$$P^2 : 1 :: \frac{d^3}{m + m^1} : \frac{1}{M}$$

Whence $m + m^1 = \frac{d^3}{P^2} M$

If p be the parallax, and a the semi-axis major of the system, both in seconds of arc, we have

$$d = \frac{a}{p} \quad \text{and hence}$$

$$m + m^1 = \frac{\left(\frac{a}{p}\right)^3}{P^2} M = \frac{a^3}{p^3 P^2} M$$

The parallax of a few of the binary stars has been determined, and the following remarks on their relative masses and distances may prove of interest to the reader.

1. We will first consider the famous binary star Alpha Centauri, which is also, as far as is yet known, the nearest of all the fixed stars to the earth. From an orbit computed by Dr. Hind in 1877, combined with a parallax of $0''\cdot928$, he found the mass of the system $1\cdot79$ times the mass of the sun, and the semi-axis major $23\cdot49$ times the earth's mean distance from the sun. Better elements of the orbit have recently been computed, and the parallax has been found to be somewhat less than that assumed by Hind. Taking the latest elements found by Dr. Elkin (period = $80\cdot34$ years, and $a = 17''\cdot20$), and his parallax of $0''\cdot75$, I find the sum of the masses = $1\cdot8686$, and the mean distance between the components = $22\cdot933$ times the sun's mean distance from the earth.

2. η Casseopeiæ. Dr. Dunér finds for this binary

a period of 176·37 years, with semi-axis major = 10″·68. Combining these elements with O. Struve's parallax of 0″·154, I find the mass of the system = 10·722 times the sun's mass, and the mean distance = 69·35. The magnitudes of the components are about 4 and 7½, so we have here a star of the 4th magnitude with a mass about six times as great as that of Alpha Centauri, a 1st-magnitude star. The elements of this system are, however, somewhat uncertain, especially the semi-axis major, which in Dunér's orbit is probably too large. A diminution of this quantity would of course diminish the resulting mass. The mass of the system computed from other orbits varies, according to Sadler, from 5·25 to 8·34 times the sun's mass. Taking the lowest estimate we have still the mass of Eta Cassiopeiæ, nearly three times the mass of Alpha Centauri!

3. *Sirius.* The well-known companion to this brilliant star was discovered by Alvan Clark in 1862, and numerous measures of position since that date prove that the *comes* is in rapid orbital motion round Sirius. The orbit was computed by Auwers, who found a period of 49·399 years and recently by Colbert, who finds a period of 49·6 years; and $a = 8″·41$. Combining Colbert's elements with a parallax of 0″·193, deduced by Gyldén from Maclear's observations, I find the mass of the system 33·62 times the sun's mass, and the mean distance =

43·57. Considering the great brilliancy of Sirius, and its immense distance from the earth—indicated by the parallax—this large value for the mass seems not improbable. Recently, however, Dr. Gill found a parallax of $0''·37$. This value gives the sum of the masses $= 4·7546$, and the mean distance $= 22·7$. Assuming that the attraction of the companion is the cause of the observed irregularities in the proper motion of Sirius, Auwers found that its mass is about one-half that of Sirius. This would make the mass of the companion—a 10th-magnitude star—greater than the mass of the sun!

4. 70 Ophiuchi. According to Schur's orbit of this interesting binary, the period is $94·37$ years, and $a = 4''·704$. These, combined with Krüger's parallax of $0''·162$, give mass of system $= 2·747$, and semi-axis major $= 29$. I have recently computed an orbit for this star, which represents recent measure more satisfactorily than those of other orbits. I find a period of $87·84$ years, with $a = 4''·50$. These, combined with the above parallax, give mass of system $= 2·777$, and mean distance $= 27·77$, not differing much from the results found from Schur's orbit. Comparing these results with those for η Cassiopeiæ, we see that, although both stars are roughly at the same distance from the earth, and of nearly the same brightness, the mass of Eta Cassiopeiæ is—on the lowest estimate—nearly double that of 70 Ophiuchi. Their densities, therefore, must be very different.

5. Castor. The parallax of this remarkable binary was found by Johnson, with the Oxford heliometer to be $0''\cdot 1984$. Dr. Doberck finds a period of $1001\cdot 2$ years, with $a = 7''\cdot 43$. As his elements agree fairly well with orbits computed by Thiele and Wilson, we may assume them to be nearly correct. From these elements and the above parallax, I find the sum of the masses $= 0\cdot 052398$ the mass of the sun, which would imply that the components are simply masses of glowing gas! If we assume that the components have the same density as the sun, the parallax must be smaller than that found by Johnson. Taking the sum of the masses as 2, the parallax would be $0''\cdot 059$. A parallax of $0''\cdot 03$ gives the sum of the masses $= 15\cdot 19$ times the sun's mass, and this value of the parallax will perhaps seem the most probable. This parallax would give for the semi-axis major of the orbit 248 times the sun's distance from the earth, and a light journey from the star to the earth of about 109 years!

6. 40 (o^2) Eridani. I recently computed an orbit for the double companion of this well-known ternary system, and found a period of 139 years, with $a = 5\cdot 99$ (*Monthly Notices*, R.A.S., March, 1886). These elements, combined with Professor Asaph Hall's parallax of $0''\cdot 223$, gives sum of masses $= 1\cdot 003$ and mean distance $= 26\cdot 86$. The magnitudes are about 9 and $10\cdot 8$. The distance of the primary star (4th magnitude) is about 82 seconds. This implies a

distance of *at least* 367 times the sun's distance from the earth, or about 12 times the distance of Neptune from the sun. It is therefore not a matter for surprise that the orbital motion of the binary pair round the principal star is exceedingly slow, and the period still unknown.

THE ABSOLUTE DIMENSIONS
OF A
STAR CLUSTER

XXII.

ON THE ABSOLUTE DIMENSIONS OF A STAR CLUSTER.[1]

THE globular star clusters are some of the most interesting objects in the heavens. They consist of thousands of minute stars, easily visible in a large telescope. It is not easy at first sight to understand on dynamical principles how an immense assemblage of bodies filling a globular space can exist in that condition without mutually interfering with each other. They cannot be at rest, for their mutual attractions would in the course of time produce a velocity in each member of the system. Possibly each of the components describes its own ellipse about the centre of gravity of the whole mass, which is probably situated near the centre of the sphere. One of the most remarkable of these wonderful objects is that known as 13 Messier, which lies between the bright stars Eta and Zeta in the constellation Hercules. Sir William Herschel estimated the number of stars it contains at 14,000,

[1] "Journal of Liverpool Astronomical Society," vol. v. p. 169.

and Admiral Smyth describes it as "an extensive and magnificent mass of stars, with the most compressed part densely compacted and wedged together under unknown laws of aggregation." This description might convey the impression to some readers that the component stars near the centre were almost or actually in contact. If, however, we consider the cluster as a sphere filled with stars, the apparent condensation at the centre is easily accounted for, and a few figures will show that if equally distributed through the sphere the component stars need not necessarily be so close as seems to be generally supposed. Mr. Proctor is of opinion that the cluster 13 Messier may not exceed in mass that of an average 1st-magnitude star. It certainly seems more probable that the components are in reality individually small, and form a sort of family, than to suppose them large suns, and merely faint from excessive distance. Let us assume the total mass of this cluster as equal to twice the sun's mass, and the density of each component the same as that of the sun. Then if $d =$ diameter of each component, we have—

$$14{,}000 \frac{\pi}{6} d^3 = 2 \times \frac{\pi}{6} (865{,}000)^3$$

whence $d = 45{,}218$ miles diameter of each component, which will be the *average* diameter, as the stars are of several sizes.

DIMENSIONS OF A STAR CLUSTER.

Secchi found that the diameter of the cluster, including outliers (not visible in small instruments), was about 8 minutes of arc. Assuming the diameter of the globular portion at 5 minutes = 300 seconds, and the parallax p of the cluster at $\frac{1}{10}$ of a second (it may possibly be much less), we have—

$$\text{Diameter of sphere} = \frac{D}{p} R = \frac{300 \, R}{0.1} = 3{,}000 \, R$$

or diameter of sphere = 3,000 times the sun's mean distance from the earth!

The volume of the sphere will therefore be—

$$\text{Volume} = \frac{\pi}{6} (3{,}000 \, R)^3$$
$$\text{} = 14{,}137{,}200{,}000 \, R^3$$

This, divided by 14,000, the assumed number of the component stars, gives $1{,}009{,}800 R^3$, or, in other words, a space for each component of 1,009,800 times the volume of a cube having the radius of the earth's orbit for its side! This volume would be equal to that of a single cube whose side $= \sqrt[3]{1{,}009{,}800 \, R^3} =$ 100·37 R, or more than three times the distance of Neptune from the sun! So that if the assumed data are at all correct, the components of this wonderful cluster may be separated from each other by a distance of over 9,000 millions of miles. At this vast distance these comparatively small bodies would exert but little disturbing influence on each other's motions, and each component would be practically free to describe its own ellipse round the common centre of gravity. A collision, however, between two of the bodies might possibly occur at rare intervals, thus perhaps giving rise to the appearance of a "temporary star" in the cluster, a phenomenon which was actually observed in 1860 in the globular cluster known as 80 Messier in Scorpio.

There is a still finer object in the Southern hemisphere, known as Omega Centauri, which is visible to the naked eye as a hazy star of about the 4th magnitude, and described by Sir John Herschel as "truly astonishing," and "beyond all comparison the richest and largest object of its kind in the heavens." The diameter of this cluster is about 20 minutes, or about four times that of 13 Messier. This implies for the same distance from the earth, a volume $= 4^3$ or 64 times greater than the Hercules cluster. There would therefore be sufficient space in Omega Centauri to contain $14,000 \times 64 = 896,000$ stars separated from each other by the vast distance found above for the components of 13 Messier. Sir John Herschel estimated the magnitudes of the small stars comprising Omega Centauri as 13 and 14. Assuming an average magnitude of $13\frac{1}{2}$, it will be interesting to compute how many stars of this magnitude will be required to give a combined light equal to that of a 4th-magnitude star, which is the stellar magnitude assigned to the cluster in Dr. Gould's "Uranometria Argentina." Taking the generally adopted "light ratio" of 2·512 we have—

$$\text{Light of 4th-mag. star} = (2{\cdot}512)^{9{\cdot}5} \times (\text{light of } 13\tfrac{1}{2}\text{-mag. star.})$$
$$= 6312 \times (\text{light of } 13\tfrac{1}{2}\text{-mag. star.})$$

so that a cluster of only 6,312 stars of the $13\tfrac{1}{2}$ magnitude would give the light of a 4th-mag. star. Sir John Herschel, however, considered that if the light of Omega Centauri were compressed into a point, and not diffused as it is over a considerable area, the cluster would probably shine as a star of about the 3rd magnitude. This would give—

$$\text{Number of stars} = (2{\cdot}512)^{10{\cdot}5} = 15856$$

a sufficiently large number of stars to be contained in a portion of the sky considerably less in area than that covered by the full moon.

Were it possible to approach this cluster to say $\tfrac{1}{100}$th of its present distance, it would then expand into a circle of about 33° in diameter, and in this circular portion of the sky would be crowded say 15,000 stars of between the 3rd and 4th magnitude —a truly magnificent spectacle.

SOME SUSPECTED VARIABLES
OF THE
ALGOL TYPE.

XXIII.

SOME SUSPECTED VARIABLES OF THE ALGOL TYPE.

THE interesting class of variable stars, of which Algol is the type, is a very rare one in the heavens, only 9 having been hitherto detected. These are in order of Right Ascension.

	PERIOD.	VARIATION IN MAGNITUDE.	DISCOVERER.
U Cephei	2·49132 days	7·2 to 9·1–9·4	Ceraski, 1880
Algol	2·86727 ,,	2·2 ,, 3·7	Montanari, 1669
λ Tauri	3·952 ,,	3·4 ,, 4·2	Baxendell, 1848
R Canis Majoris	1d. 3h.	5·9 ,, 6·7	Sawyer, 1887
S Cancri	9d. 11h. 37·75m.	8·2 ,, 9·8–11·7	Hind, 1848
δ Libræ	2d. 7h. 51m. 20s.	4·9 ,, 6·1	Schmidt, 1859
U Coronæ	3d. 10h. 51m. 14·6s.	7·6 ,, 8·8	Winnecke, 1869
U Ophiuchi	0d. 20h. 7m. 41·6s.	6·0 ,, 6·7	Sawyer, 1881
Y Cygni	1d. 12h.	7·1 ,, 7·9	Chandler, 1886

Owing to the fact that in these remarkable variables all the light variations take place in the course of a few hours, while for the remainder—and much the longer portion—of the period, the light of the star remains constant, it will be seen that the discovery of variables of this class is a matter of no small difficulty. We may at some time chance to observe the minimum of a star of this type, but from ignorance of its period we cannot tell when to expect another minimum, and consequently a long time may elapse before we can confirm our suspicion. It may be argued that probably few stars exist having this very peculiar type of variation, but still only 9 stars among the thousands known to astronomers seems a very small number indeed, and it is quite possible that this small number may be really due more to the difficulty of observation than to the paucity of such stars in the heavens.

The following notes on some stars which may possibly be variables of this very interesting type may perhaps induce amateurs to observe them occasionally. A passing glance at the stars referred to on clear nights might perhaps be rewarded some night by an interesting discovery. The stars are given in order of Right Ascension.

1. ν Cassiopeiæ R.A. 0h. 42m., N. 50° 19' (1880). Rated once as 7th mag., and once at 5th mag., by Lalande. It is 5th-mag. in Harding's Atlas. Argelander and Heis also make it 5; the *Durchmusterung* 5·2; it was measured 5·00 at Harvard, and 4·93 at Oxford. As all the estimates are in close agreement —with exception of Lalande's 7th mag.—the star may possibly be a variable of the Algol type.

2. 54 Andromedæ ($=\phi$ Persei) R.A. 1h. 36·1m., N. 50° 5' (1880). Rated once as 6th mag., and once 4th

mag. by Lalande (Nos. 3,116–17). It was estimated 4th mag. by Argelander and Heis; 4·1 in *Durchmusterung*: measured 4·24 at Harvard, and 4·29 at Oxford.

3. 7 Arietis. R.A. 1h. 49m. 9s., N. 22° 59'·5 (1880). This star was rated once as 7th mag. and once 5th mag. by Lalande (3,540–41). Piazzi in 1798 observed it to increase from 8th mag. to 6th mag. in an interval of four days, and again in 1803. His words are: "Quator dierum intervallo ab 8a. ad 6a. magnitudinem stellam hanc transiise mihi visum. Non inde tamen inter variabiles eam referre anderem." As other observations show that the star is *not* a short-period variable like η Aquilæ or δ Cephei, the increase of light from 8th mag. to 6th mag. in the short space of four days seems strongly to point to variations of the Algol type. In 1850 Argelander made observations of the star to confirm, if possible, the supposed variability, but without result. It is still possible, however, that it may be an Algol variable, and an occasional glance at the star might some night be rewarded by an observation of a minimum. I have recorded sixteen observations of the star from Nov. 1875 to Nov. 1886. These only vary from 5·8 to 6·2, and this apparent small fluctuation may possibly be due to errors of observation, the proximity of the star to λ Arietis (a 5th-mag. star) rendering comparisons with other stars somewhat difficult and uncertain. It was

rated 6th mag. by Heis, and was measured 5·90 with the photometer at Harvard.

4. ξ Persei. R.A. 3h. 51m. 12s., N. 35° 27′ (1880). Rated once as $5\frac{1}{2}$ mag., and once as $7\frac{1}{2}$ mag. by Lalande. Argelander and Heis make it 4; the *Durchmusterung* 4·2. It was measured 4·06 at Harvard, and 4·31 at Oxford. If the star was not obscured by cloud when Lalande rated it $7\frac{1}{2}$, it may possibly be a variable of the Algol type.

5. 65 (b) Geminorum. R.A. 7h. 22m. 24s., N. 28° 10′ (1880). Rated once $5\frac{1}{2}$, and once $8\frac{1}{2}$ by Lalande. Bessel made it 7th mag.; all other observers 5 or 5–6. It was measured 5·13 at Harvard, and 4·97 at Oxford (or 5·07 in the Harvard Scale)—a close agreement. My observations, 1880–1885, show the light of the star constant, or nearly so. Lalande's $8\frac{1}{2}$ mag. would therefore seem to point to variation of the Algol type.

6. ζ Ursæ Majoris. R.A. 13h. 19m. 6s., N. 55° 33′ (1880). Madler found the companion to this bright star invisible on April 18, 1841. About an hour afterwards it was again visible, and he suggested that the companion might be a variable of the Algol type, but with a much longer period. As he was using a telescope at the time, the close companion (at 14″ distance), and not Alcor (the naked-eye companion) seems to be referred to. Telescopic observers would do well to examine this star occasionally, and compare its brightness with that of Alcor.

7. λ Serpentis. R.A. 15h. 40m. 36s., N. 7° 44′ (1880). On Sept. 5 (?), 1877, I observed that this star was exactly equal in brightness to the 6th-mag. star Lalande, 28,716 (about 1° south of a Serpentis). On April 21, 1878, I found λ distinctly the brighter of the two. My observations since that date show that the light of Lalande, 28,716 (6·1 mag. in the "*Uranometria Argentina*") is practically constant, and that of λ Serpentis apparently so also. The observation of Sept., 1877, would therefore seem to show that λ is probably a variable of the Algol type. It was rated 4th mag. by Ptolemy and Al-Sufi, 4–5 by Argelander and Heis, 4½ by Lalande, 4 by Harding, and 4·8 at Cordoba. It was measured 4·35 at Harvard, and 4·68 at Oxford. As 4·35 in the Harvard scale corresponds to 4·25 in that of Oxford, there is a difference of 0·43 magnitude between the photometric measures. On April 7, 1886, I estimated λ Serpentis 0·1 mag. less than ι Serpentis.

8. θ Serpentis. R.A. 18h. 50m. 15s., N. 4° 2′·8. Strongly suspected by Montanari to be variable, but Pigott found it 1783 to 1785, always of the 4th magnitude. It was rated 4th mag. by Ptolemy and Al-Sufi; 4–3 by Argelander and Heis. The Cordoba estimates vary from 4·1 to 4·6, and Dr. Gould thinks there are strong indications of variability in one of the components, the magnitudes of which he gives as 4·5 and 4·7. The components were measured 3·91 and 4·23 at Oxford, or a difference of 0·32 mag.,

agreeing well with the Cordoba estimates of relative brightness; but on one occasion at Harvard, July 15, 1878, a difference of 1·4 magnitude was noted between the components.

9. ϵ Pegasi. R.A. 21h. 38m. 18s., N. 9° 20′ (1880). This star, which is generally rated 2 or 2½ magnitude, Schmidt found unusually faint in a perfectly clear sky, Nov. 5, 1847. Signs of variation were also observed at Cordoba. Seidel, from photometric determinations, believes it to be variable, and Schwab's observations point to variations with a period of about twenty-six days. Schmidt's observations in Nov., 1847, seem to suggest variability of the Algol type.

THE POSITIONS
OF THE
PLANES OF BINARY STARS.

XXIV.

ON THE POSITIONS OF THE PLANES OF BINARY STARS.[1]

THE number of double stars in which change has been detected in the positions of the components now probably amount to nearly 1,000. In many cases, however, the apparent change is due to proper motion in one or both stars. For instance, in 45 Geminorum, Struve 1516 (A.B.), and Struve 2120, the large observed angular change is due to rectilinear motion in one of the components, and in the case of Struve, 1819, for which an orbit has been computed by Casey (period 340·1 years) it has been shown by the German computer Berberich (*Astronomische Nachrichten*, No.2,518) that all the measures are satisfactorily represented on the assumption of uniform rectilinear motion. In a large number of cases, however, physical connection undoubtedly exists, although in most of them a sufficiently large

[1] From the "Journal of Liverpool Astronomical Society," vol. vi. p. 52.

arc of the orbit has not yet been described to enable an orbit to be computed with any approach to accuracy.

Of 498 stars given as binary, or probable binary, in the "Handbook of Double Stars," by Messrs. Crossley, Gledhill, and Wilson, I find that 172 lie in or near the Milky Way, a large proportion, if we consider that most of these binaries are brighter than the 8th magnitude, and that the excessive number of stars in the Milky Way is chiefly due to faint stars.

Of the pairs certainly known to be binary, the orbits of about fifty have now been computed, and attempts have been made to ascertain whether any relation exists between the positions of the planes of their orbits and that of a fixed plane, such as the plane of the Milky Way. A list showing the positions of the poles of thirty-three orbits was published by Dr. Doberck in 1882 (*Astronomische Nachrichten*, No. 2,433). To make the list as complete as possible I have computed the positions of the poles of orbits computed since the date of Dr. Doberck's paper. (See Appendix, Note L.) I have omitted τ Cygni, of which the published elements (*Astronomische Nachrichten*, No. 2,749) are most probably erroneous (due to faulty observations), and Struve 1819, in which—as mentioned above—the change is possibly due to rectilinear, and not orbital, motion.

Sir John Herschel gives the position of the poles

of the Milky Way as R.A. 12h. 47m., and + 27° for the North pole, and R.A. 0h. 47m. and — 27° for the South pole, or—

$$192°, +27° \text{ and } 12°, -27° \text{ nearly},$$

and this agrees closely with Dr. Gould's determination given in the "*Uranometria Argentina*" (p. 371), derived from observations in the Southern hemisphere.

Comparing these positions with the positions of the poles of the forty-eight orbits now computed, I find that there is no marked tendency to parallism with the plane of the Milky Way, the following being the nearest approach to coincidence with the pole of the Galactic plane :—

	R.A.	DECL.
ω Leonis	206°	+ 34°
ξ Bootis	182°	+ 31°
36 Andromedæ	9°	— 29°

Comparing, however, the positions of the binary star poles with the Milky Way itself, I find that in twenty-eight orbits out of the forty-eight, one of the alternative poles lie in or close to the Milky Way, indicating that the plane of the orbit is possibly at right angles to the Galactic plane. The possibility, however, of the other alternative plane being the correct one renders any definite conclusion on the point uncertain. For the following binaries, however, I find that *both* alternative planes lie in or near the Milky Way, and of course in these cases there can be no doubt (assuming the computed orbit to be correct), that the plane of the real orbit is at right angles, or nearly so, to the plane of the Milky Way.

	R.A.	DECL.	R.A.	DECL.
Sirius	63°	+ 25°	155°	− 49°
70 Ophiuchi	316°	+ 44°	227°	− 41°
O. Struve 400	356°	+ 52°	269°	+ 18°
δ Cygni	300°	+ 82°	296°	+ 7°
λ Cygni	359°	+ 83°	305°	− 13°
42 Comæ	103°	+ 10°	283°	− 10°
44 Bootis	89°	+ 56°	249°	− 19°
γ Coronæ Borealis	10°	+ 61°	203°	− 53°

Of the above stars, the first five lie in or near the Milky Way, 42 Comæ lies close to the pole of the Galaxy, and in this case—as might be expected—the plane of the orbit passes through the earth, the inclination being 90°. In γ Coronæ, the inclination is about 85°, and in 44 Bootis over 70°, and neither are very far distant from the Galactic pole.

Of the 96 poles (48 orbits) 60 lie between 150° and 300° R.A., showing, perhaps, some tendency to a plane, of which the pole is in R.A. 10 hours to 20 hours, and not very far from the equator, chiefly to the north of it. This relation was pointed out to me by Mr. Monck.

In the case of 42 Comæ, ζ Herculis, and η Coronæ, there seems to be an approach to parallelism in a plane whose pole is in R.A. 282°, and Decl.

about 4° S., and in σ Coronæ, O. Struve 298, and λ Ophiuchi to a plane whose pole is in R.A. 284° and and 16° N. These positions lie in the Milky Way. A few others show a similar relation, but not in so marked a degree as those just quoted.

If we consider our own sun as a binary star with a very small companion (Jupiter), the plane of the orbit (the ecliptic, or nearly so) is inclined at a high angle to the plane of the Milky Way, and so is the sun's equator, its axis of rotation pointing nearly to π Draconis, which is not far from the Milky Way. Mädler having investigated in 1838 the probable position of the plane of the orbit in 51 physical systems came to the conclusion that there exists a sort of stellar equator to which the planes of the orbits are almost parallel, and of which the north pole has the following position—

R.A. + 73°   Decl. + 52°

From an examination of the poles of the orbits computed up to the present I cannot find any evidence in favour of Mädler's hypothesis. It may be added, however, that the position of the pole found by Mädler lies close to the Milky Way, so that his "stellar equator" would be at right angles, or nearly so, to the Galactic plane, a fact he does not appear to have noticed.

STELLAR PHOTOGRAPHY.

XXV.

STELLAR PHOTOGRAPHY.

SEVERAL attempts were made during the last fifty years to obtain photographs of the stars and other celestial bodies, but owing to the difficulties connected with the wet-plate process, these attempts did not prove very successful. The first photograph of a star was made at Harvard Observatory (U.S.A.) some forty years ago, when the bright stars Vega and Castor were, after considerable trouble, successfully photographed. For many years after this the progress made in this branch of astronomy was very slow, but of late years, owing to the introduction of the dry-plate process, attention has again been directed to the subject, and with wonderful success. Photographic charts of portions of the sky have now been obtained by two different methods; one by using an ordinary camera mounted on a stand and driven by clockwork, so as to follow the stars in their apparent diurnal course round the earth, and the other by placing the photographic plate in the focus of a large telescope also driven by clockwork. The former method has been successfully employed by the Rev. T. E. Espin, F.R.A.S., by means of a camera specially constructed for the purpose by Mr. (now Sir) Howard Grubb, the eminent Dublin optician. The second method has been used with still greater success by the Brothers Henry, the eminent astronomers of the Paris Observatory. By the aid of extra sensitive dry plates placed in the focus of a large telescope, and exposed to the sky for one hour, they have obtained very beautiful photographic charts, which show thousands of faint stars hitherto invisible to astronomers using the largest telescopes in existence. This result may seem puzzling at first sight, but a little consideration will show how it is that faint stars invisible to the eye impress their images on the photographic plate. When the eye looks through a telescope many faint stars are seen by glimpses which cannot be held steadily even on the finest nights. After long gazing the eye wearies, and if the effort to see these faint points of light is persisted in, they soon fade away into the dark background of the sky. Not so, however, with the photographic eye, as it may be called. The longer the plate is exposed, the greater impression will be made, but even with very sensitive plates an exposure of an hour is necessary to obtain an image of the faintest stars. With so long an exposure the brighter stars will, however, be much "over exposed," and will be expanded into discs of different sizes, proportional to the brightness of the star. In this way an accurate chart is obtained, showing the bright and faint stars, the faintest stars being almost points. As might be expected, stars of a reddish colour give much smaller discs than white stars. At the Paris Observatory, three separate photographs of each portion of the sky—each with an exposure of an hour—are taken, and these being compared, any small accidental specks which may exist in the plates, and which might otherwise be mistaken for stars, are detected. Some remarkable results have already been obtained. In a photographic chart of the Pleiades, made by MM. Henry, it has been found by comparison with an eye chart previously made by M. Wolf with a large telescope, that, while the eye chart contained 671 stars, the photographic map shows no less than 1,421 stars! The great nebula in Andromeda, showing the temporary star which suddenly appeared in Aug., 1885, has been photographed, and also the remarkable spectrum of the new star in Orion discovered by the present writer in Dec., 1885. A spiral nebula ha been discovered by photography surrounding the star Maia in the Pleiades, the existence of which was previously unsuspected. This nebula has since been seen with the giant 30-inch refractor of the Pulkowa Observatory, but it would probably have escaped detection for many years had not photography revealed its existence. In a photograph taken at Harvard in Nov., 1885, this nebula is also visible, but it was supposed to be due to a defect in the plate, till its true nature was shown by a comparison with the Paris photographs. A photograph of the region in Orion, in which the new star was discovered in Dec., 1885, was also taken at Harvard about five weeks before the discovery, and on this photograph no trace of the new star is visible, showing that its rise to the 6th magnitude must have been rather rapid.

An International Congress of Astronomers was held at Paris in 1887, to arrange a plan for forming a photographic chart of the whole heavens, and it was arranged that the chart should include all stars to the 14th magnitude, and that there should also be a series of plates with a shorter exposure, showing stars to the 11th magnitude inclusive, for the purpose of forming an accurate catalogue of stars to that magnitude, of which the heavens contain about about $1\frac{1}{2}$ millions. The chart of stars to the 14th magnitude will be useful in the search for variable stars, minor planets, and planets beyond Neptune, if any such exist, and for the investigation of the laws which govern the distribution of the stars in space, and their distance from the earth. When this great work has been accomplished, we shall be able to hand down to the astronomers of future generations an exact picture of the heavens as they now exist, and in the words of an eminent English astronomer, himself famous for his work in stellar photography, "the records that the future astronomer will use, will not be the written impressions of dead men's views, but veritable images of the different objects of the heavens recorded by themselves as they existed."

We may assume the total number of stars visible in the largest telescopes at about 70 millions. Now the present population of the earth is about 1,400 millions, so we have the curious, and probably to some very unexpected, result that, for every star *visible* in the heavens, there are 20 human beings on the earth! If we assume the distance of Sirius (as indicated by Gyldén's parallax) at 100 billions of miles, there would be sufficient space for all the visible stars in the heavens, if placed in a line between the earth and Sirius!

THE ZODIACAL LIGHT.

XXVI.

THE ZODIACAL LIGHT.[1]

THE Zodiacal Light is a cone-shaped or lenticular beam of light which makes its appearance at certain times of the year above the eastern horizon in the mornings before the dawn, and above the western horizon after sunset in the evening, remaining visible long after twilight has ceased. The phenomenon requires no instruments for its observation, and may best be seen with the naked eye.

The light is generally assumed to be due to a sort of nebulous envelope surrounding the sun, extending

[1] Published in *Naturalists' Monthly* for November, 1887. In case any reader may think that this article is merely a copy of a chapter on the Zodiacal Light in Mr. Westwood Oliver's recently published work "Astronomy for Amateurs," I think it well to state here that the chapter in that book was compiled by me. This will appear from the fact that Mr. Oliver's book was not published till 1888. Both articles are, of course, merely compilations, and have no claim to originality whatever. It may be confidently stated, however, that most of the details here given respecting the Zodiacal Light will not be found in any other popular work on astronomy.

beyond the earth's orbit, and consisting of finely-divided matter of some sort, which shines either by reflected sunlight, or by inherent light of its own, due to electrical or chemical action. The hypothesis that it is a terrestrial appendage, and not a solar one has been shown by Proctor to be inconsistent with its appearance and position as seen in northern latitudes.

There have been numerous observations of the Zodiacal Light recorded by experienced observers, but it has been remarked by Schmidt that all the observations made in the year 1855 to 1868 seem to add little or nothing to our knowledge of the position and true character of this mysterious phenomenon. The first regular observations appear to have been made by Commander Jones in the years 1853-1855, while engaged on the United States Japan Expedition, and to this able observer seems to be due the discovery that the apparent position of the light varies with the inclination of the ecliptic to the horizon.

The Zodiacal Cone—as it may be termed to distinguish it from other allied phenomena, which have been called the Zodiacal Band and the Gegenschein — is, according to Lewis, the only part of the phenomenon which varies in appearance. It has often been described in popular works on astronomy, but is frequently misrepresented, especially in pictures intended to represent its appearance, but which generally show it much brighter and more clearly defined than it is usually seen, at least in northern latitudes. The brightness of the Zodiacal Light depends upon the time of year. It is most visible when the ecliptic makes the greatest angle with the horizon, and is therefore best seen by an observer in this country in the evenings in February and March, and in the mornings about October. As amateurs often find a difficulty in perceiving the Zodiacal Light from not knowing what to look for, and when to look for it, observations may be most suitably made at the above-mentioned periods of the year. A clear evening or morning should be chosen, with the moon absent, although feeble moonlight does not overpower it. The last traces of twilight must have died away in the evening, or the observation must be made before the commencement of the dawn, if the inexperienced eye is to detect it as a distinct object. Its appearance, then, is that of a spindle-shaped light rising from the horizon at a steep inclination to that plane. Its light is always brightest near the centre, and fades away very gradually towards the edges. According to Lewis, the axis of greatest brightness lies south of the axis of symmetry. The lower edge of the cone is generally more distinctly defined than the upper. Jones found that the light was deficient on the south side, when seen from a place north of the equator, and on the north side when seen from the south.

This may be explained by atmospheric absorption acting more efficiently in reducing the light on the side of the cone which is nearer to the horizon. The Zodiacal Cone is brightest near the sun, but still sufficiently bright at a distance of 50° or 60° to be quite conspicuous to a trained eye. The apex of the light occasionally reaches to a distance of 100° from the sun. In the brighest visible part of it, the light is several times as bright as the brightest parts of the Milky Way visible in northern latitudes. On two occasions—Feb. 12, 1877, and Feb. 21, 1879—it was found by Lewis sufficiently bright to cast a shadow! On the latter night snow covered the ground, on which distinct shadows were visible. In the tropics where the twilight is very short the light is very bright, and visible almost every clear night. In Northern India the present writer has seen it shining with great brilliancy, and not to be overlooked by the most casual observer; and even in the West of Ireland it was very conspicuous in March, 1887, and Feb., 1888. Jones' observations seems to show an elongation of the Zodiacal Light towards the east as the evening advances; but Searle points out that this apparent extension may be really due to an effect of contrast caused by an increase in the darkness of the sky for a long time after twilight has ended, and possibly also to an increase in the sensitiveness of the observer's eye, which may take place more gradually than is generally supposed.

Tacchini, on Dec. 15 and 29, 1874 and Serpieri on Feb. 22, 1875, saw "the *central light* forming an internal cone with a well-marked and distinct outline on the fainter background of diffused light." The latter observer found the Zodiacal Light generally faint in the second half of the year 1878, although it had been most splendid in February, and particularly on Feb. 20th, when it was more brilliant than the Milky Way.

Many people, on first seeing the phenomenon, mistake it for a continuance of twilight from its ill-defined outline, but it may be easily distinguished by the fact that the twilight extends along the horizon for a considerable distance, and only reaches up a short distance in the sky, whereas the Zodiacal Light at the periods of the year named, makes an angle of about 60° with the horizon in our latitude, and is comparatively narrow.

As has been said the Zodiacal Light extends beyond the earth's orbit, and should therefore be visible round the whole sky. Many observers have noticed an extension of this sort, forming a zone of faint light, considerably fainter than the Zodiacal Cone itself, and which has been called the Zodiacal Band. This band has been observed by Backhouse, Barnard, Brorsen, Lewis, and Schmidt; but Searle thinks that his own observations indicate it to be a sidereal, and not a Zodiacal phenomenon at all. Backhouse can always see it under fairly favourable atmospheric conditions, stretching right across the sky, except from about the Pleiades to the Præsape, where it is merged in the light of the Milky Way. He finds that it cannot be clearly observed when at all near the horizon, as the light of the sky increases downwards, and so extinguishes the dark space that would otherwise be visible below the Zodiacal Band. He can never see it in the southern portion of the Zodiac, owing to its low altitude in the North of England. It would seem that keen sight is necessary to observe this very faint band as, according to Lewis, it is one of the faintest objects in the heavens, being considerably fainter than the faintest portion of the Milky Way. Lewis, who has seen it well, finds that his sight is sufficiently acute to enable him frequently to see twelve stars in the Pleiades with the naked eye. He finds that the band is somewhat brighter in the centre than at the edges. It cannot of course be seen when it crosses the Milky Way, and is best observed when the Galaxy is on or near the horizon. As might be expected this faint band of light disappears in moonlight, although its visibility in the presence of the moon has, it is said, been recorded on two or three occasions! Barnard finds the breadth of this band to be usually 4° to 5°. Although the Zodiacal Band on the whole becomes fainter as its distance from the sun increases, yet in the region directly opposite the sun its brightness revives again to a considerable degree. This brighter portion was named by Brorsen, who discovered it, the Gegenschein (in English the Counter Glow). The Gegenschein is always found to lie, within 2° or 3° of a point in the heavens, almost directly opposite the sun's place. It is brighter than the Zodiacal Band, although always much fainter than any of the brighter parts of the Milky Way. The brighter portion of this patch of light is probably circular, and about 7° in diameter, although it has occasionally been observed as apparently elliptical with the longer axis parallel to the ecliptic. It was independently discovered by Backhouse in 1875, and again in 1883 by Barnard, who found a faint illumination of the sky in that part of the Zodiac which is on the meridian at midnight. The latter observer describes it as "a roundish mass of hazy light," about 10° to 15° degrees in diameter, "and though probably very slightly so, it is not perceptibly brighter in the middle." Observations by Searle, 1878 to 1884, show a marked tendency to place the Gegenschein in north latitude. This result is confirmed by Lewis, who finds that it always lies about 2° north of the ecliptic, not a single observation placing it south of that line. Heis also agrees in fixing its position north of the ecliptic, and so does Barnard, who, however, thinks that more accurate observation would place it *exactly* opposite the sun. Searle thinks the fact may be accounted for by atmospheric absorption, but the absence of any observations in the southern hemisphere renders it difficult to decide this point. It is not easy to frame any hypothesis which will satisfactorily account for the appearance of the Gegenschein, but on the meteoric theory it could be explained by assuming such a law for the phases of the meteors that their brightness would rapidly increase as they approached opposition.

The Zodiacal Light — like all faint indefinite objects—is seen very differently by different people, as it requires practice to enable its fainter portions to be observed, and eyes vary greatly in power. In order to see it satisfactorily it will be necessary to exclude all bright light from the eyes, and it cannot be well seen in a town where there is smoke illumined by gaslight, or where the electric light is used, as in the city of Boston (U.S.A.), where Searle finds it no longer possible to make any useful observations.

Owing to the fact that the brightest portion of the light is seen only near the horizon, and that most of it is very faint, its appearance is greatly affected by atmospheric conditions. For this reason it is not easy to determine whether its light is variable or constant. Backhouse states that he has never noticed any changes of brightness other than can be accounted for by atmospheric variations. He thinks it probable, however, that the Gegenschein varies in form and size.

Photometric comparisons of the light with that of the Milky Way will perhaps be necessary to determine whether it really varies in brightness or dimensions. Some observers have noticed momentary flashings in it; but probably these are merely subjective phenomena similar to stellar scintillation.

The real nature of its substance still remains a mystery. Practically it is a feeble extension of the Solar Corona, although probably existing under very different conditions to that portion of the corona visible in total eclipses of the sun. Searle suggests that a portion at least of its light may be due to sunlight reflected from very minute planets which may possibly accompany the asteroids in large numbers; and if we suppose a number of meteoric particles diffused through the Solar System, and reflecting light irregularly, it may be shown mathematically that an appearance resembling the Zodiacal Light, with an indefinite vertex would be the result. Sir John Herschel held a similar opinion. Observations show that the axis is not precisely on the ecliptic. Backhouse, from his own observations, finds the probable position of the ascending node somewhere about longitude 35°, with an inclination of about 1·7°. Houzeau found, from a discussion of 58 observations by various observers, that the longtitude of the ascending node is about 2° with an inclination of about 4°; but owing to the difficulty of making sufficiently delicate observations, it can hardly perhaps be considered proved that there is any fixed inclination. To determine this accurately observations in the southern hemisphere, and still better near the equator, would be necessary, as the atmospheric absorption towards the horizon will necessarily shift the axis more or less towards the north as seen in northern latitudes. Cassini was of opinion that the axis of the Zodiacal Light lies in the plane of the sun's equator, and this idea is partly supported by observation. It also seems probable on theoretical grounds, "for it is possible that the rotation of the sun indicates the fundamental plane of the Solar System, if we accept the ordinary nebular hypothesis for its formation, more correctly than can be done by the revolution of the known planets" (Searle).

It was stated by Angström that he had seen the auroral line in the spectrum of the Zodiacal Light, but it is now considered more probable that there was some feeble auroral light in the sky at the time of his observation, which he did not notice, as other observers have failed to detect any line. During the aurora of May 2, 1877, the Zodiacal Light was also visible, and Lewis found that the Zodiacal Cone gave "a faint short continuous spectrum, brightest near its least refrangible end." "It was very faint throughout, and could only be seen through a wide slit," too wide to permit the Fraunhofer dark lines to appear. He thinks that his spectroscopic observations point to reflected sunlight as the source of the light of the Zodiacal Cone. The aurora gave a much longer spectrum "though of the same pale greenish colour."

Searle finds from his own observations that there exists "a faint permanent band of light" about 2° or 3° in width, closely south of Beta and Eta Virginis, nearly parallel to these stars, and reaching as far as Spica. It appears, however, that there is a slight relative abundance of small stars all along the ecliptic in this region, which may possibly, he thinks, account for the faint band referred to. Whether this applies to the fainter telescopic stars must be left, perhaps, to photography to decide.

Geelmuyden remarks that if we suppose the Zodiacal Light to bear the same relation to the general meteoric matter of the Solar System, that the comets of short period bear to the comets in general, there should be some relation between the plane of Jupiter's orbit and that of the Zodiacal Light, and he finds that such a coincidence actually exists.

The appearance of the Zodiacal Light in tropical regions is thus described by Du Chaillu, the African explorer: "Then, as if to give a still grander view to the almost enchanting scene, the Zodiacal Light rose after the sun had set, increasing in brilliancy, of a bright yellow colour, and rising in a pyramidal shape high in the sky, often so bright that it overshadowed the brightness of the Milky Way and the rays of the moon, the beautiful yellow light gradually diminishing towards the apex. It cast a gentle radiance on the clouds round it, and sometimes formed almost a ring, but never perfect, having a break near the meridian; at times being reflected in the east with nearly as much brilliancy, if not as much as in the west, and making me almost imagine a second sunrise. April and May were the months when the light showed itself in its greatest brilliancy. On April 13, 1865, the glow coming from the west was so bright that it totally hid the Milky Way in the principal part of its course. I could only distinguish it above the Sword of Orion; the glow was the brightest below the planet Mars, and the base of the pyramid reached on the south the part of the Milky Way at the foot of the Cross."

The Zodiacal Light was noticed in England by Childrey about the year 1660, and that it was a familiar object in Shakspeare's time may perhaps be inferred from the passage in "Romeo and Juliet"—

> "Yon light is not daylight, I know it, I:
> It is some meteor that the sun exhales."

ON THE INFINITY OF SPACE.

XXVII.

ON THE INFINITY OF SPACE.

THE question whether space is infinite or limited in extent is an interesting one, and has given rise to numerous speculations. The idea of infinite space is, to our finite faculties, inconceivable, and it has been aptly described by one writer as "a sphere whose centre is everywhere and circumference nowhere." It seems equally impossible to imagine that space should have a limit in any direction. For a limit to any space implies a bounding surface, and we cannot conceive of a boundary anywhere, even at a distance far beyond that of the smallest star visible in our largest telescopes, without imagining something beyond that boundary. We are thus placed on the horns of a dilemma. Boundless space and a limited universe seem both beyond the mind of man. It has been argued by some astronomers that the number of the stars must be limited, for on the supposition of an infinite number uniformly scattered through space, it would follow that the whole heavens should shine with a uniform light, probably equal to that of the sun. To explain why this is not the case it has been suggested that the light of the most distant stars is absorbed by the luminiferous ether which is supposed to fill all space, and to form the medium by which the light waves are transmitted from the stars to the earth. This theory may possibly account for the extinction of the light of many very distant and comparatively small stars, but it will scarcely explain why the visible stars are so limited in number, for limited they certainly seem to be. In the photographic chart of the whole heavens now in preparation at various observatories, the total number of stars shown on the plates will most probably not exceed 70 millions. This must be considered a very limited number indeed, if we remember that the present population of the earth is about 1400 millions. If we assume the parallax of Sirius at one-fifth of a second, I find that the whole of the 70 millions of stars could be placed in a straight line between the earth and Sirius without touching each other (assuming that the *average* diameter of each does not much exceed that of the sun). It seems to me that the difficulty may be met by supposing that all the stars, nebulæ, and clusters visible to us—either with large telescopes or by the aid of photography—constitute one system or universe, in fact one vast cluster in space similar to the Magellanic clouds in the southern heavens, and that there are other universes external to ours, the light of which can never reach the earth, owing either to their vast distance, or to

ON THE INFINITY OF SPACE. 235

the absence of any ether or other medium in the void between capable of conveying the rays of light to any point in our universe.

Let us first consider the former hypothesis. If we assume the distance of the faintest star visible by photography to be such that its parallax is, say only $\frac{1}{1000}$ of a second of arc, or $0''\cdot001$, and that the *average* distance between the component stars of our universe is such that the parallax of one as seen from the other is $0''\cdot 2$ (which seems to be a reasonable supposition). Then further, assuming that the average distance between two universes bears the same (or nearly the same), ratio to the diameter of each universe, that the mean distance between the components of each universe bears to the diameter of each component, we can compute the probable distance of the nearest external universe from our system.

For putting the unit of circular measure $(206,265'') = c$
and the radius of the earth's orbit $= R$, we have
Radius of visible universe $= 1000\, c\, R$
and average distance between components $= 5\, c\, R$
Assuming the diameter D of each component such that $R = 100\, D$
(which is roughly correct in the case of the sun), we have
Radius of visible universe $= 100{,}000\, c\, D$
and Diameter $= 200{,}000\, c\, D$
and average distance between components $= 500\, c\, D$
Then if $x =$ distance between the separate universes, we have the proportion
$$D : 500\, c\, D :: 200{,}000\, c\, D : x$$
and $\therefore x = 100{,}000{,}000\, c^2\, D$
or $x = 4{,}254{,}525{,}022{,}500{,}000{,}000\, D$,

a distance which light would require millions of years to traverse; so that if such universes really exist we should possibly know nothing of their existence, as their light would probably not yet have reached the earth. If we look upon space as infinite, this does not appear to be an extravagant supposition.

Let us now consider the second hypothesis. As far as we can ascertain anything respecting the nature of the so-called ether which seems to pervade our universe, and without which (or some such medium), it is evident that the light of even the nearest star could never reach our eyes, it appears probable that it is a substance incapable of existence except in some way connected with matter or motion. If this be the case, we may assume that in the spaces between the separate universes or galaxies, there is an *absolute* vacuum through which the light of the stars can never penetrate, and which for ever isolates the light of each universe from its surrounding neighbours. On this theory it would follow that, as the component stars of our universe thinned out, towards its outskirts the luminiferous ether would thin out too, and at a certain distance from the earth would cease to exist altogether. We should then reach an *absolute* vacuum, across which the waves of light could not be propagated, and which would cut off from our view any external galaxies which might exist in the infinity of space beyond. What the exact consequences would be of this thinning out of the ether on the rays of light from stars in our universe it is not an easy matter to decide. It was considered by Fresnel that all reflection of light was due to a change in the density of the ether, which he thought existed inside solid bodies as well as outside them. If this idea is correct it seems probable, on the above theory, that the rays of light from the stars composing our universe would be reflected back from the verge of the vacuum, and that a considerable increase in the general light of the sky would result. If we suppose our universe to be roughly globular in shape, we may consider the reflecting vacuum as forming the internal surface of a hollow sphere. Supposing the earth situated near the centre of this sphere, it is evident that the only ray of light from any star which could reach the centre of the sphere by direct reflection is that which strikes the sphere at right angles to a tangent plane. This reflected ray will evidently return along the radius of the sphere, and will, therefore, be intercepted by the star itself. On the other hand, rays passing along the diameter towards the opposite side of the sphere will be intercepted by the earth, and in this case there will be no reflection. Other rays will of course be reflected at various angles and points, but few of these can reach the earth. It was, however, maintained by M'Cullagh that the ether had the same density both inside and outside a solid body, and experiments made by eminent physicists to decide between the rival opinions of Fresnel and M'Cullagh led unfortunately to contradictory results. Assuming, however, the accuracy of Fresnel's hypothesis, and the consequent reflections of the light rays from the supposed inter-Galactic vacuum, it seems probable that after a number of these reflections had taken place the light vibrations would eventually cease, and the energy thus apparently dissipated may perhaps be converted into heat, thus tending in the course of ages to raise the general temperature of the ether, and preserve the great principle of the conservation of energy.

APPENDIX.

APPENDIX.

NOTES ON THE PLANETS.

NOTE A.

MERCURY.

The mass of the planet has been variously estimated from $\frac{1}{3182843}$ of the sun's mass by Rothman to $\frac{1}{7836440}$ by Von Asten. Le Verrier found from the perturbations of Venus $\frac{1}{7310000}$, and Buckland from researches on the motion of Encke's comet the high value of $\frac{1}{2668700}$.

NOTE B.

VENUS.

Le Verrier found the mass of the planet (from perturbations of Mars) at $\frac{1}{412150}$ of the sun's mass, and Hill from the movement of the node of Mercury's orbit $\frac{\text{Sun's Mass}}{427170}$.

NOTE C.

MARS.

Mass according to Le Verrier, $\frac{1}{2812526}$, and

according to Hall (from observations of the satellites), $\frac{1}{3093500}$ of the sun's mass. Period of rotation according to Proctor is 24h. 37m. 22·735s., and according to Bakhuyzen, 24h. 37m. 22·66. Seidel found that Mars in opposition = 2·97 times light of Vega. Zöllner found for Mars a stellar magnitude of — 2·25 or $2\frac{1}{4}$ magnitudes higher than an average star of the 1st magnitude.

Note D.

THE ASTEROIDS.

Le Verrier has computed from the perturbations of Mars that the total mass of all the asteroids between the mean distances of 2·20 and 3·16 cannot exceed one fourth of the mass of the earth. According to Stone, the diameters of the principal asteroids are probably about as follows: (1) Ceres, 196 miles; (2) Pallas, 171; (3) Juno, 124; (4) Vesta, 214; (5) Astræa, 57; (6) Hebe, 92; (7) Iris, 88; (8) Flora, 61; (9) Metis, 76; and (10) Hygeia, 103 miles.

Note E.

JUPITER.

The apparent equatorial diameter of Jupiter is, according to Hough and Colbert, 39″·764 and the ellipticity $\frac{1}{16\cdot78}$. The mass is according to Doubjago, $\frac{1}{1046\cdot25}$, and according to Schur, $\frac{1}{1047\cdot252}$ of the sun's mass. The earth's mass adopted by Le Verrier is $\frac{1}{324439}$ of sun's mass, and according to Newcomb, $\frac{1}{322800}$. Hough finds the following formula for the rotation, from observations of the red spot—

$$9\text{h. }55\text{m. }33\cdot2\text{s. }+ 0\cdot18\text{s. }\sqrt{t}$$

where t is the number of days since Sept. 24, 1879. Sir J. Herschel found Jupiter's light $= \frac{\text{Moon's Light}}{6620}$, and Bond gives $\frac{\text{Moon}}{6430}$. Seidel found Jupiter 8·24 times as bright as Vega (a Lyræ). Zöllner found Jupiter 10·48 times a Lyræ, and its stellar magnitude — 2·52, or 2·52 magnitudes brighter than an average star of the 1st magnitude. If we call the mean motions of the three interior satellites n', n'' n''', the following relation exists—

$$n' - n'' = 2(n'' - n''')$$
$$\text{or } n' - 3n'' + 2n''' = 0$$

Also if L', L", L''' be the mean longitudes, we have always—

$$\text{L}' - 3\text{L}'' + 2\text{L}''' = 180°$$

Note F.

SATURN.

The most ancient mention of this planet is a Chaldean observation recorded by Ptolemy, which was made in the year B.C. 228. According to Le Verrier the mass of Saturn is $\frac{1}{3520\cdot8}$ of the sun's mass. Meyer makes it $\frac{1}{3182\cdot9}$, and Hall $\frac{1}{3478\cdot7}$. The mass of the ring is, according to Tisserand $\frac{1}{820}$ of Saturn's mass. Bessel found $\frac{1}{118}$, but Hall thinks this is much too great. Tisserand finds the mass of Titan $= \frac{1}{11000}$ of that of Saturn. Kirkwood finds for the mean motions of the four interior satellites the relation—

$$5(n_1 - n_2) + (n_5 - n_2) + 4(n_4 - n_2) = 0$$

The "great inequality" in the motion of Jupiter and Saturn depends on the exact equality which exists between twice the mean motion of Jupiter and five times the mean motion of Saturn. Its period is 929 years.

Note G.

URANUS.

The apparent diameter is, at the mean distance, according to Vogel, $3''\cdot624$, and according to Kaiser, $3''\,62$. The mass is, according to Newcomb, $\frac{1}{22138}$ of the sun's mass, $\frac{1}{22000}$ according to Holden, and $\frac{1}{22682}$ according to Hall, quantities in fairly close agreement.

Note H.

NEPTUNE.

Apparent diameter, according to Kaiser, $2''\cdot87$. The mass of Neptune is, according to Newcomb, $\frac{1}{19380}$ of the sun's mass, and according to Hall, $\frac{1}{19092}$, or somewhat greater than that of Uranus.

Galle estimated the stellar magnitude of the planet as 8, and Grünewald 7.

BINARY STARS.

Note I.

The following are some details of binary star orbits recently computed by the author [1]:—

1. β Delphini. Long known as a wide double star, the companion being of the 11th magnitude, and distant about 34″ from the bright star. In 1873 the eminent observer Burnham discovered that the primary was a very close double, and a few years' observations sufficed to show that it was a binary in rapid motion. I have computed an orbit for this star, and find a period of 30·91 years, with eccentricity = 0·337 and inclination of the orbit to the plane of projection = 59° 20′, the apparent semi-axis major of the real ellipse being only 0·517 of a second of arc. The elements represent the measures fairly well from 1874 to 1884. The orbit has also been computed by the Russian astronomer Doubjago, who finds a period of 26·07 years, with eccentricity = 0·3567, and semi-axis major = 0″·55. ("*Proccedings* of the Royal Irish Academy," 1886.)

---

[1] Details of these calculations have been published in the *Proceedings* of the Royal Irish Academy, "*Monthly Notes* of the Royal Astronomical Society," and the *Astronomische Nachrichten*.

2. γ Coronæ Australis. For this interesting southern binary star, Jacob found a period of 100·80 years, and Schiaparelli 55¼ years. I have computed the orbit, and find a period of 81·78 years, with inclination = 47° 26', eccentricity = 0·322, and semi-axis major = 1"·885. This orbit represents recent measures better than the others, but will probably require revision. ("*Monthly Notices* of the Royal Astronomical Society," January, 1886.)

3. OΣ 234. R.A. 11h. 24m. 20s., N., 41° 58' (1880). For this close and difficult binary star, I find a period of 63·45 years, with eccentricity = 0·3629, inclination = 47° 21', and semi-axis major = 0"·339. Some of the measures are very discordant, and could not possibly be represented by any elliptic orbit. My orbit represents the other measures from 1843 to 1880 fairly well for so close a pair. ("*Proceedings* of the Royal Irish Academy," 1886.)

4. 40 (o²) Eridani. I have computed an orbit for the double companion of this well-known triple star, and find a period of 139 years, with eccentricity = 0·1362, inclination = 76° 20', and semi-axis major = 5"·99. The angles from 1783 to 1883 are fairly represented by this orbit, but the distances are not satisfactory. This orbit will require revision when further measures are obtainable.

5. 14 (i) Orionis. For this binary I find a period of 190·48 years, with eccentricity = 0·2465, inclination = 44° 57', semi-axis major = 1"·22, and time

of periastron passage = 1959·05 A.D. This orbit represents the measures from 1844 to 1887 fairly well. Some of the recorded measures in recent years are somewhat discordant. ("*Monthly Notices* of the Royal Astronomical Society," March, 1887.)

6. *O.* Struve 400. R.A. 20h. 6m. 14s., N., 43° 35'. For this close and difficult pair I find a period of 170·37 years, with eccentricity = 0·669, and semi-axis major 0"·59. Some of the measures are very discordant, and the orbit will require revision. ("*Monthly Notices* of the Royal Astronomical Society," April, 1887.)

7. Struve 1757. R.A. 13h. 28m. 29s., N., 0° 16' 6". For this binary I find a period of 276·92 years, with eccentricity = 0·4498, inclination = 40° 56', and semi-axis major = 2"·05. This orbit represents the measures from 1825 to 1887 fairly well, but there seems to be some disturbing element at work in this system. ("*Monthly Notices* of the Royal Astronomical Society," June, 1887.) An orbit was previously calculated by the American computer Carey, but this does not represent recent measures satisfactorily.

8. 12 Lyncis. I have computed an orbit for the close pair of this well-known triple star, and find a period of 485·8 years, with eccentricity = 0·229, and semi-axis major = 1"·64, the periastron passage taking place in 1716 A.D. This orbit represents all the measures from 1782 to 1887 fairly well. Admiral Smyth predicted (Bedford Catalogue, p. 156) that,

owing to the fixity of the third star, the orbital motion of the close pair would "bring the three stars into a straight line in about half a century." This prediction has now been fulfilled (*Astronomische Nachrichten*, No 2,802).

9. *p* Eridani. For this southern binary I find a period of 302·37 years, with eccentricity = 0·674, inclination = 38° 31', semi-axis major = 6"·96, and periastron passage 1823·55 A.D. The observations from 1825 to 1886 are fairly well represented by this orbit. ("*Monthly Notices* of the Royal Astronomical Society," November, 1887.)

10. 70 (*p*) Ophinchi. As none of the orbits calculated for this famous binary star represent recent measures at all well, I have computed an orbit, and find a period of 87·84 years, with eccentricity = 0·4912, inclination = 58° 28', position angle of line of nodes = 120° 5', node to periastron 171°·45', semi-axis major = 4"·50, and periastron passage 1807·65. This orbit represents closely all the measures of position angle from 1781 to 1887, but the distances not so well.

ALGOL.

Note J.

At maximum Algol is not quite equal to a star of the 2nd magnitude. Sir John Herschel estimated

APPENDIX.

it 2·62; it is 2·31 in "The Harvard Photometry," and 2·40 in "The Uranometria Nova Oxoniensis;" and at minimum it is certainly brighter than the 4th magnitude. According to Schönfeld's observations, the variation of light is included between the magnitudes 2·2 and 3·7. Taking the "light ratio" as 2·512 (the value now generally adopted) we have—

$$L_{2\cdot2} = (2\cdot512)^{1\cdot5} \; L_{3\cdot7} = 3\cdot981 \; L_{7}''$$

or Light at maximum = 3·981 × Light at minimum; hence, if r and r' be the radii of the bright star, and dark occulting satellite respectively, we have—

$$\left(\frac{r'}{r}\right)^2 = \frac{3\cdot981 - 1}{3\cdot981} = 0\cdot749$$

$$\text{and} \quad \frac{r'}{r} = 0\cdot865$$

Schönfeld gives the light at maximum as 20·8, and at minimum 5·6, whence—

$$\left(\frac{r'}{r}\right)^2 = \frac{20\cdot8 - 5\cdot6}{20\cdot8} = 0\cdot7307$$

$$\text{and} \quad \frac{r'}{r} = 0\cdot854$$

According to the late Professor Schmidt's observations, the fluctuations of light extend over $9\frac{1}{4}$ hours; and from photometric measures at Harvard, Professor Pickering finds the duration of the light variation to amount to ten hours. Adopting the latter result, we have, assuming the orbit to be circular—

$$\frac{2(r-r')}{2\pi a} = \frac{15}{4129}$$

and $\quad \dfrac{2r'}{2\pi a} = \dfrac{300}{4129}$

a being the radius of the orbit of the dark body round the centre of the bright body, whence $\dfrac{r}{a} = 0.2396$, $\dfrac{r'}{a} = 0.2282$, and $\dfrac{r'}{r} = 0.952$. Professor Pickering, in his investigation of the variation of Algol, finds $\dfrac{r'}{r} = 0.764$; "and assuming the brightness of Algol equals that of our sun," he finds $r = 0''.003$, and radius of orbit $0''.014$. This gives $\dfrac{r}{a} = 0.214$, and $\dfrac{r'}{a} = 0.163$. The value $\dfrac{r'}{r} = 0.764$ gives for the loss of light. $\left(\dfrac{r'}{r}\right)^2 = 0.5836$, but this does not agree with the variation observed by Schönfeld. Maxwell Hall deduces the interesting result that the density of Algol $= 0.25$, or one-fourth that of water, and says, "In the case of the components of Algol, as Mr. Lockyer argues in the case of the sun, we are undoubtedly dealing with masses of gas."[1] (See "Observatory," June and July, 1886).

STELLAR PARALLAX.
Note K.

Let the radii of the parallactic circles be R and r,

---

[1] See p. 183, where I have deduced a similar result with reference to the components of the binary star Castor.

and half the angle at c, a. Then the angle A G E $=$ a, and A E $=$ R $-$ r. Also, let the distance K F $=$ d. Then we have—

$$\text{Tan } a = \frac{AE}{EG} = \frac{R-r}{R+d-r} = \frac{R-r}{R-r+d}$$

$$\therefore (R-r)\tan a + d \tan a = R-r$$

whence $R - r = \dfrac{d \tan a}{1 - \tan a} =$ relative parallax.

BINARY STAR ORBITS.

Note L.

The following are the formulæ of computation—

$$\sin D = \cos i \sin \delta \pm \sin i \cos \delta \sin \Omega$$
$$\cos D \sin (a - A) = \pm \sin i \cos \Omega$$
$$\cos D \cos (a - A) = \cos i \cos \delta \pm \sin i \sin \delta \sin \Omega$$

where a and δ are the right ascension and declination of the star, i the inclination of the orbit to the plane of projection, Ω the position angle of the line of nodes, and A and D the right ascension and declination of the pole of the orbit; the double values being due to the uncertainty which necessarily exists as to which part of the true orbit is on the positive side of the plane of projection or in front of it, or in other words, whether the positive angle Ω refers to the ascending or descending node of the orbit referred to the plane of projection or the background of the sky. By means of the above formulæ I have computed the positions of the poles of the following recently published orbits—

	Computer.	R.A.	Decl.	R.A.	Decl.
Struve 2107	Casey	336°	+46°	205°	—19°
,, ,,	Berberich	300	+15	201	+24
φ Ursæ Majoris	Casey	178	+65	133	— 2
δ Cygni	Behrmann	300	+82	296	+ 7
μ Draconis	Berberich	255	+55	no alternative pole, as $i = 0°$	
β Delphini	Dubjago	365	+21	256	— 5
ζ Sagittarii	Gore	277	+28	361	—83
Σ 1757	,,	200	+41	204	—41
14 (i) Orionis	,,	86	+52	67	—36
O Σ 234	,,	247	+65	147	0
O Σ 400	,,	356	+52	269	+18
12 Lyncis	,,	173	+43	44	+31
p Eridani	,,	53	—24	300	—64
λ Cygni	(unpublished)	359	+83	305	—13
δ Equulei	Wrublewsky	232	+25	28	+ 2
61 Cygni	Peters	236	+30	13	+ 2

Note M.

Herr L. Struve determines the position of the point towards which the Solar System is moving, to be—

R.A. 273° 21′   Decl. + 27° 19′

from a discussion of the proper motion of 2,509 stars. The probable rate of motion per annum he considers to be about $4\frac{1}{3}$ radii of the earth's orbit. He also determines the constant of precession as

50″·3514. Nyrén found 50″·3269 ("Journal of Liverpool Astronomical Society," April, 1888).

ON THE MAGNITUDES OF DOUBLE STARS.

There seems to be considerable doubt with some telescopic observers as to the correct magnitudes to be assigned to the components of certain double stars. For instance, in the well-known double γ^2 Andromedæ, the components have been variously rated 4 and 5, 5·5 and 6·8, and even 8·5 and 9 mag.! Yet (Webb says) "variation has not been suggested." The following considerations may help to clear up this uncertainty—

Taking a "light ratio"[1] of 2·512, as assumed by Professor Pritchard in his photometric measures of the brighter stars, and that now generally adopted by astronomers—

Let L_m represent the light of a star of Magnitude m,
L_{m+1} the light of a star one magnitude fainter,
L_{m+2} that of a star two magnitudes fainter,

and so on. Then we have generally—

$$L_m = (2·512)^n L_{m+n}.$$

---

[1] The "light ratio" is "the ratio of the intensities of light which shall define the meaning of 'difference of a single magnitude' between the light of two stars." Thus a star of 1st magnitude is assumed to be 2·512 times the light of a 2nd magnitude star, and so on.

In the case of a double star we may calculate the combined light of the component stars as follows—

Taking L_m and L_{m+n} as the light of the components,
$$L_m = (2\cdot512)^n\, L_{m+n} \text{ and } \therefore L_{m+n} = \frac{L_m}{(2\cdot512)^n}$$

and as the light of the combination—which call L_c—will evidently be the sum of the lights of the components, we have

$$L_c = L_m + L_{m+n} = L_m + \frac{L_m}{(2\cdot512)^n}$$
$$= \frac{L_m\{(2\cdot512)^n + 1\}}{(2\cdot512)^n}$$

Now if $x =$ difference of magnitude between the combination and the brighter component, we have—

$$L_c = (2\cdot512)^x\, L_{c+x}$$

If we assume the light of the brighter component $= 1$, we have—

$$\frac{(2\cdot512)^n + 1}{(2\cdot512)^n} = (2\cdot512)^x$$

Now if $n = 0$, or the components are equal, we obtain

$$(2\cdot512)^x = 2, \text{ whence } x = 0\cdot75.$$

Therefore in a double star consisting of two components of equal brilliancy, the magnitude of the combination will be obtained by *deducting* 0·75 from the magnitude of either component, and conversely, if we know the magnitude of the combination, the numerical magnitude of each component will be found by *adding* 0·75 to the magnitude of the combination.

Similarly if n = 1, we have—

$$(2·512)^x = \frac{3·512}{2·512} = 1·4$$

whence x = 0·365.

Let us take a few examples of double and binary stars.

(1) γ^2 Andromedæ. The components of this close double have been variously estimated by different observers from 4 and 5 by O. Struve to 8·5 and 9 by Secchi. Professor Pritchard measured it 4·86 with the "wedge" photometer (1882·693). Assuming that the components differ by one magnitude, their magnitudes would be 5·22 and 6·22, or, taking a difference of 1½ magnitude, they would be 4·88 and 6·38.

(2) ζ Aquarii. The components of this binary star are usually rated 4 and 4½. The star was estimated 3·5 at Cordoba ("*Uranometria Argentina*," p. 207). The components will therefore be 3·5 + 0·5 = 4, and 4·5, so that the assumed magnitudes are correct.

(3) Castor. Struve rated the components 2·7 and 3·7. Pritchard measured the star 1·48. The components would therefore be 1·53 + 0·36 = 1·89, and 2·89.

(4) η Orionis. Mags. 4, 5. This star was measured 3·66 at Oxford. The components will therefore be 4·02 and 5·02.

(5) α Piscium. Mags. 2·8 and 3·9, Struve; 5 and 6, Schmidt. Webb says (*Cel. Objects*, p. 378), "Both magnitudes very variously given; but Fl. remarks with always about 1 magnitude difference." Dr. Gould estimated the star 3·8. The components would therefore be 4·16 and 5·16. They were measured 3·71 and 4·70 at Oxford (1882·623). The Harvard measure is 3·99, which would make the components 4·36, and 5·36, but the star is suspected of being slightly variable.

(6) γ Virginis. Magnitudes 3, 3 Struve; 4, 4 Smyth. It was measured 2·67 at Oxford, and therefore the magnitude of each component will be 2·67 + 0·75 = 3·42. The Harvard measure is 2·84, which would make each component 3·55; but here again variable light has been strongly suspected in one of the components.

(7) κ Herculis. In the *Astronomical Register* for July, 1884, Mr. Johnson says he finds the components of this wide double star "very nearly equal in magnitude." On April 10, 1884, I estimated the star 5·0 by comparison with ω Herculis (4·8 Gould). The components would therefore be 5·75 magnitude each. The star is, however, a suspected variable. It was rated 4–5 by Al Sufi, 6 magnitude by Lalande and Harding; 5 magnitude by Argelander;

5–6, Heis. It was measured 5·04 at Oxford, and 4·81 at Harvard. The magnitudes of the components in the *Durchmusterung* are 5·5 and 7·0.

ON THE COLOURS OF THE COMPONENTS OF BINARY STARS.[1]

The following interesting relation between the magnitudes and colours of the components of binary stars has been previously pointed out,[2] but as I have recently detected it independently, and as the relation is not generally known, it may prove of interest to the reader.

1. When the magnitudes of the components of a binary star are equal, or approaching equality, the colours are generally the same, or similar.

2. When the magnitudes of the components differ considerably, there is also a considerable difference in colour.

The following table includes most of the double stars certainly known to be binary. They are arranged in order of right ascension.

CLASS I. COLOURS OF COMPONENTS SIMILAR.

Star.	Magnitudes.		Colours.
Struve 2	6·3	6·6	A yellow, B deeper yellow.
,, 13	6·6	7·1	Both white or yellowish.

[1] "Journal of Liverpool Astronomical Society," vol. vi. p. 55.
[2] By Professor Holden in the "American Journal," June, 1880, and also, I believe, by Dr. Doberck.

Star.	Magnitudes.		Colours.
p Eridani	6¼	6¼	Both yellow.
Struve 73	6·2	6·9	Golden.
,, 186	7·2	7·2	White.
,, 228	6·7	7·6	White (Struve, Dembowski and Secchi).
7 Tauri	6·6	6·7	Both white or yellowish.
12 Lyncis	5·2	6·1	Both yellowish white.
Struve 1037	7·1	7·1	Both yellowish or white.
Castor	3	3·5	Both white or greenish.
Struve 1126	7·2	7·5	White, ashy.
ζ Cancri	5	5·7	Both yellow or pale red.
Struve 1338	7	7·2	Both white.
,, 1348	7·5	7·6	Both white.
ω Leonis	6·2	7	"A yellow, B yellower."
ξ Ursæ	4	5	"Subdued white, greyish white."
o Struve 234	7	7·4	Both white.
γ Virginis	3	3	Both yellowish.
42 Comæ	6	6	Both white or yellow.
Struve 1781	7·8	8·2	Yellowish white.
α Centauri	1	2	Both yellow or reddish.
η Coronæ	5·2	5·7	Both yellow.
μ Bootis	6·7	7·3	Both greenish white.
o Struve 298	7	7·3	Both yellow.
ξ Scorpii	4·9	5·2	White or yellowish.
μ Draconis	5	5·1	Both white.
μ² Herculis	9·5	10·5	Both white.
τ Ophiuchi	5	5·7	Both white, yellowish, or pale red.
γ Cor. Australis	6	6	Both full yellow.
61 Cygni	5·3	5·9	Both golden.
ζ Aquarii	4	4·1	"Flushed white, creamy."

Class II. Colours of Components Different.

Star.	Magnitudes.		Colours.
η Cassiopeiæ	4	7·6	Yellow, purple.
φ Andromedæ	4·9	6·5	Yellow, green.
Struve 208	6·2	8·4	Yellow, ash.
ι Cassiopeiæ	4·2	7·1	Yellow, blue.
84 Ceti	6	10	White, lilac.
γ Ceti	3	6½	Yellow, blue.
Struve 422	6	8·2	Yellow, blue.

APPENDIX.

Star.	Magnitudes.		Colours.
2 Camelopardali	5	7·4	Yellow, blue.
Sirius	1	10	Brilliant white, deep yellow.
38 Geminorum	5·4	7·7	Yellowish, bluish.
ε Hydræ	3·8	7·8	Yellow, blue.
σ² Ursæ	5	8·2	"Flushed white, sapphire blue."
ι Leonis	4·8	7·9	Yellowish, blue.
35 Comæ	5	7·8	Yellowish, blue.
25 Can. Venat.	5	7·6	White, blue.
Struve 1777	5·8	8·2	"Yellow, very blue."
,, 1837	7·1	8·7	Pale yellow, greenish.
ε Bootis	3	6·3	{ A yellow, or reddish. B blue or green.
ξ Bootis	4·7	6·6	Yellow, "reddish purple."
γ Cor. Borealis	4	7	Greenish white, purple.
λ Ophiuchi	4	6·1	Yellow, bluish.
ζ Herculis	3	6·5	Yellowish, reddish.
Struve 2107	6·5	8	Yellowish, bluish.
70 Ophiuchi	4·1	6·1	Yellow, purple (var?)
Struve 2434	8·4	10·3	White, blue.
δ Cygni	3	7·9	Pale yellow; sea-green or blue.
ε Draconis	4	7·6	Light yellow, blue.
τ Cygni	5·6	7·9	Yellow, blue.
52 Pegasi	6·2	7·7	White, red.
π Cephei	5·2	7·5	Yellow, purple.
ο Cephei	5·2	7·8	Very yellow, very blue.

Most of the details in the above table are derived from the "Handbook of Double Stars," by Messrs. Crossley, Gledhill, and Wilson. A few well-known binaries have been omitted, notably δ Equulei, 85 Pegasi, and ζ Sagittarii, for which I could not ascertain the colours of the components. The magnitudes are chiefly those given by Struve. In the highly-coloured stars the estimates of magnitude may possibly have been influenced to some extent by the colour, but this will not, I think, materially affect the general result.

CLASSIFICATION OF THE VARIABLE STARS.[1]

In the following classification of the variable stars, I have adopted the classes proposed by Professor Pickering, of Harvard College Observatory, viz. :—

Class I. Temporary Stars.
,, II. Stars undergoing large variations of light in periods of several months.
,, III. Irregularly variable stars, undergoing but slight changes in brightness, as α Orionis.
,, IV. Variable stars of short period, like β Lyræ, δ Cephei, and 10 Sagittæ.
,, V. Algol stars, or those which at regular intervals undergo sudden diminutions of light lasting for a few hours only.

I have given the colours of the stars where these have been well observed.

Class I.

Temporary Stars.

No. of stars, 9.
Greatest magnitude when first seen, >, *Nova* Cassiopeiæ, 1572.
Least ,, ,, ,, 7, *Nova* Andromedæ, 1885.
Colours noted, 2 " white "—*Novæ*, 1572 and 1604 (afterwards " ruddy ").
3 " yellow "—P Cygni, *Nova* 1866, and *Nova* 1876.
1 " glaring red "—Nova Ophiuchi, 1848.

All the stars in this class—with the single excep-

[1] From "Journal of Liverpool Astronomical Society," vol. v. p. 23.

tion of *T* Coronæ (Nova, 1866)—appeared in or near the Milky Way. This would not, however, hold good for a few of the earlier "temporary" stars, of which the positions have not been recorded with accuracy, and which are not included in the above.

CLASS II.

Stars undergoing considerable variations of brightness in periods of several months.

LENGTH OF PERIOD, DAYS.	NO OF STARS.	GREATEST VARIATION IN MAG.	LEAST VARIATION IN MAG.	COLOUR.
100 to 120	2	—	—	1 very reddish.
120 to 145	4	5·5	1·0	Red and yellow-red.
145 to 175	6	5·2	1·4	Yellow-red to red.
175 to 200	7	5·1	1·3	{ 1 yellow-red. { 1 orange-red.
200 to 225	11	6·3	2	Chiefly reddish.
225 to 250	6	6±	1	Chiefly yellow.
250 to 275	9	over 5	2·2	Chiefly red-yellow.
275 to 300	14	over 5	1·9	Chiefly reddish.
300 to 325	17	7·2	1·8	Chiefly red.
325 to 350	15	7·8	2·8	Chiefly very red.
350 to 375	14	6·8	0·9	Chiefly reddish.
375 to 400	7	over 5 ?	3·3?	Chiefly reddish.
400 to 425	8	8·8	4 ?	Chiefly red.
425 to 450	5	7±	2·3 ?	All remarkably red.
450 to 475	3	6·2	3±	2 red, 1 reddish.
475 to 500	2	4·1	2·3	Both remarkably red.
500 to 600	0	—	—	
600 to 700	1	6±	—	Red (S Cassiopeiae)
Over 700	2	4±	3±	1 reddish
Many Years	1	9 ?	—	η Argûs.

It will be seen from the above table that the greatest variation in stars of this class (with regular periods) is found among those having periods of 400 to 425 days. The largest number of stars is found among those with periods of 300 to 325 days.

Class III.

Irregularly Variable Stars, undergoing—as a rule—but slight changes of brightness.

No. of stars, 14.

Greatest variation ...... 2 magnitudes ∓ (R Monocerotis).
Least variation ...... 0·4 magnitude (α Orionis).

Sub-Class IIIa.

Considerable Variation.

No. of stars, 3.
Greatest variation .... 7·2 magnitude.

The colours of the stars in Classes III. and IIIa. are three white, five little or no colour, two yellow-red, five red, one "scarlet," and one "plum colour" or "ruddy purple."

Class IV.

Variable Stars of Short Period.

LENGTH OF PERIOD, DAYS.	NO OF STARS.	GREATEST VARIATION IN MAG.	LEAST VARIATION IN MAG.	COLOUR AND REMARKS.
0 to 5	6	1·4	0·4	White or yellowish.
5 to 10	10	2·0	0·8	Chiefly yellow.
10 to 15	2	1·1	0·8	Yellow.
15 to 20	2	1·7	—	Reddish.
20 to 25	0	—	—	
25 to 30	1	1·4	—	Yellow. T Monocerotis.
30 to 35	2	2±	1·5	No colour.
35 to 40	0	—	—	
40 to 50	0	—	—	
50 to 75	3	3·8	1·1	

It will be seen that the largest number of stars of this class have periods of five to ten days, and are chiefly yellow. All the short-period variables, with the single exception of W Virginis (period 17·27 days) lie in or near the Milky Way, and it is the only one of the class which has been noted as " reddish."

Sub-Class IVa.

Stars with short periods, but somewhat irregular.

LENGTH OF PERIOD, DAYS.	NO OF STARS.	GREATEST VARIATION IN MAG.	LEAST VARIATION IN MAG.	COLOUR AND REMARKS.
30 to 50	2	1·2	0·8	Red.
50 to 125	1	1·2	—	— g (30) Herculis.

Class V.

Algol Type.

No. of stars, 9.

Greatest variation ...... 3·5 magnitudes (S Cancri).
Least   ,, ... 0·7   ,,   (U Ophiuchi).

The general colour of stars in this Class is white, or only slightly yellow. The star with the greatest variation (S Cancri) has the longest period, and the star with the smallest variation (U Ophiuchi) has the shortest period, but the variation in the others is not proportional to the period. Chandler finds that the shorter the period of the star, the higher is the ratio which the time of light variation bears to the whole period. For a full list of stars of this class see paper on " Some Suspected Variables of the Algol Type."

In addition to the above classes, Espin thinks that his own observations indicate a new class of Variable Stars with the following characteristics :—

Period	Irregular.
Variation	1½ magnitude.
Spectrum	IV. Type.

and to this class he considers the following stars belong :—19 Piscium ; Birmingham 277, 521, 535, 541 ; Espin 116, 154, and perhaps Birmingham 85, 120, 121, 240, 290, 418, 464, 483, and 502. The stars of this class are subject to rapid and uncertain changes of brightness ("Journal of the Liverpool Astronomical Society," vol. vi. p. 63).

www.ingramcontent.com/pod-product-compliance
Lightning Source LLC
Chambersburg PA
CBHW032212230426
43672CB00011B/2529